THE CHARCOAL DILEMMA

THE CHARCOAL DILEMMA

*Finding sustainable solutions
for Brazilian industry*

F. ROSILLO-CALLE, M. A. A. de REZENDE,
P. FURTADO and D. O. HALL

Practical Action Publishing Ltd
25 Albert Street, Rugby,
Warwickshire, CV21 2SD, UK
www.practicalactionpublishing.com

First published in 1996
Transferred to digital printing in 2008

A catalogue record for this book is available from the British Library & Library of Congress

ISBN 978-1-85339-322-8 Paperback
ISBN 978-1-78044-436-9 Digital book

Citation: Rosillo-Calle, F. (1996) *The Charcoal Dilemma: Finding a sustainable solution for
Brazilian industry*, Rugby, UK: Practical Action Publishing
https://doi.org/10.3362/9781780444369

Since 1974, Practical Action Publishing has published and disseminated books and information
in support of international development work throughout the world. All print editions are
produced and distributed via ethical and sustainable print on demand global facilities.

Practical Action Publishing is a trading name of Practical Action Publishing Ltd (Company Reg.
No. 01159018 | VAT 880 9924 76). All profits are covenanted back to its parent group, Practical
Action (Charity Reg. No. 247257).

The views and opinions in this publication are those of the author and do not represent those of
Practical Action Publishing Ltd or its parent charity Practical Action. Reasonable efforts have
been made to publish reliable data and information, but the author and publisher cannot assume
responsibility for the validity of all materials or for the consequences of their use.

Typeset by J&L Composition Ltd, Filey, North Yorkshire, UK

The manufacturer's authorised representative in the EU for product safety is Lightning Source
France, 1 Av. Johannes Gutenberg, 78310 Maurepas, France. compliance@lightningsource.fr

Contents

Acknowledgement   viii
Introduction   xi

1. Brief History of Charcoal   1
    1.1   General background   1
    1.2   Charcoal in Brazil   2

2. The Charcoal-based Industrial Sector   6
    2.1   Main features of the iron and steel industry   6
    2.2   Overall charcoal consumption in the pig-iron and other
         industrial sectors   8

**3. Raw Material for Charcoal Production: From Native Forests
to Forest Plantations**   10
    3.1   History of forest plantations   10
    3.2   Silvicultural aspects   13
    3.3   Eucalyptus varieties and wood densities   14
    3.4   Seedling generation and planting methods   15
    3.5   Tree spacing and cutting age   15
    3.6   Biodiversity preservation and insect control   16
    3.7   Yields   17
    3.8   Afforestation programmes for charcoal production in Minas
         Gerais   18
    3.9   Socio-economic factors   20
    3.10 Legal aspects of afforestation   21

4. Technical Aspects of Charcoal Production   22
    4.1   Fundamentals   22
    4.2   Charcoal-making technology   23
    4.3   Masonry kilns in commercial charcoal production   24
    4.4   Material balance and charcoal yield   27
    4.5   Charcoal versus coke   29

5. Charcoal Production Costs   31

**6. The Future Challenge: The Need for Sustainable and Rational
Use of Native Forests**   35
    6.1   Carajas   35
    6.2   The sustainable forest management concept   37
    6.3   Sustainable Forest Management Project of 'Fazenda'
         Descoberta   39

7. Environmental Factors in Charcoal Production and Use   44
7.1   General aspects   44
7.2   Coke versus charcoal   44
7.3   The CO_2 factor   47

8.   General Perspectives   48
8.1   General considerations   48
8.2   Research and development needs   50
8.2.1 Forestry   51
8.2.2 Charcoal production   51
8.3   By-products recovery   52

9.   Summary and Conclusions   56
9.1   Charcoal production   56
9.2   Charcoal costs   57
9.3   Sustainable Forestry Management Projects (SFMPs)   58
9.4   Environment   58

10.   References   61

Tables
1.1   Evolution of charcoal consumption in the main
       industrial sectors in Brazil, 1978–91.   66
2.1   Classification of the Brazilian pig-iron and steel
       industry by group in 1992.   67
2.2   Industrial consumption of charcoal in Brazil, 1988–92.   67
3.1   Afforestation with fiscal incentives in Brazil, 1967–86.   68
3.2   Afforested area by small- and medium-scale farmers
       programme: Fazendeiro Florestal, MG.   68
3.3   Employment in the charcoal-based industries, 1989
       and 1992.   69
4.1   Main characteristics of a typical industrial charcoal kiln.   70
4.2   Main characteristics of charcoal and coke.   71
4.3   Main characteristics of charcoal for blast furnaces
       of Belgo-Mineira, MG, Brazil.   72
5.1   Average charcoal prices in Brazil for 1992 and 1982–92.   72
5.2   Estimated approximate cost of charcoal from
       well-managed forests, in Minas Gerais.   73
5.3   Summary of estimated cost of charcoal from Amazon
       forests on a non-sustainable basis.   74
5.4   Summary of costs of charcoal production from
       sustainable forestry management project, Fazenda
       Descoberta.   75
7.1   Summary of CO_2 balance from charcoal and coke-based
       pig-iron production.   75

Appendices

1. Brief Summary of Brazil's Basic Statistics   76
2. Some Problems with Measuring Wood and Charcoal   78

Acknowledgements

This book draws a considerable amount of information from extensive field visits to forest plantations, charcoal-making sites, iron and steel plants, and personal contacts with scientists, foresters, and charcoal-makers. It has developed with the help of a great many people. We would like to thank all of them but there are too many to list; we offer our apologies for this.

We would especially like to thank Jose Mauricio Belo Elian, Director Industrial of Companhia Siderurgica Vale do Pindare, and Luiz Carlos Cardoso Vale of Del Rey Servicos de Engenharia Ltda, for their kind support during the visit to Acelandia and Fazenda Descuberta. We would also like to thank the following people: Antonio Carlos Ferreira, Coordinator Tecnico, and Rubens Teodoro da Costa, Director Superintendente, both from Acesita Energetica; Clovis Pupo Nogueira, Guilherme Dias de Freitas, and Jose Octavio Benjamin of Mannesmann FL-EL Florestal Ltda; Fernando Carraza of the Universidade Federal of Minas Gerais; Jose Luis de Magalhaes Neto, Director-Presidente of Cia. Agricola e Florestal Santa Barbara-CAF and also Lima Goncalves, the Director de Florestas Elesier; Luis Macedo, Consultant, Belo Horizonte; Paulo Roberto Paixao Bretas of the Secretaria Municipal de Planejamento of Belo Horizonte; Renaldo S Sampaio from the Secretaria de Estado de Ciencia, Tecnologia e Meio Ambiente of MG; Salim Jordy Filho of Florestas Rio Doce S.A. We also thank Paulo Santos de Assis and Rolf Georg Fuchs of Usina Barreiro, Belo Horizonte, of the Mannesmann Group. All photographs in the text and on the cover are courtesy of Dr. Frank Rosillo-Calle/Biomass Users Network. Finally, we thank Sarah Hemstock of Kings College London for her help in editing our work. This work was supported in part by grants to the Biomass Users Network, which we gratefully acknowledge.
Frank Rosillo-Calle is a Research Fellow. He obtained his doctorate from the University of Aston, UK, with an investigation of Brazil's bioethanol programme. He has published extensively on biomass energy and biomass-related areas, with over 30 articles and books, many of which refer to Brazil. Maria Emilia Rezende is Director of BIOCARBO and a charcoal and by-products expert. She was a biomass research co-ordinator at ACESITA. Pompilio Furtado is a Consulting Engineer. He was Director of Technological Services and Energy Co-ordinator of CETEC, the Minas Gerais State Technology Center. David Hall is a Professor of Biology. His degrees are from

South Africa (agriculture) and California (plant physiology). His main interest has centred on basic and applied aspects of photosynthesis, particularly biomass for fuels and chemicals. He has published over 300 articles and books, many related to biomass.

Introduction

Issues in the production and use of charcoal in Brazil have wide international, environmental, and biomass resource implications. Both industrial and developing countries looking to the large-scale use of biomass as a modern energy source should examine carefully the Brazilian experience.

This book examines the history of charcoal production and its chief industrial applications: pig-iron and steel making. It compares charcoal with coke as a thermal and reducing agent, and it considers the main charcoal production areas, raw materials, (native and plantation forests), sustainable forestry and plantation practices, charcoal-making technology, production costs, use of by-products, and socio-economic factors, and examines future prospects. It argues for economic and environmental sustainability as the means to ensure the future of the charcoal and charcoal-based pig-iron and steel industry.

Brazil is a world leader in the use of renewable energy. In 1992, the country's primary energy production was about 152Mtoe (million tonnes oil equivalent), of which nearly 112Mtoe (74 per cent) came from renewable sources – about 66Mtoe (43 per cent) was from hydro, and 47Mtoe (31 per cent) from biomass (see Appendix 1). An important feature of biomass energy in Brazil, unlike that in many other countries, is the use of biomass in large-scale industrial applications. Ethanol from sugarcane is used as a substitute for gasoline, for example, charcoal for the pig-iron, steel, cement, and other metallurgy industries, and bagasse for electricity generation.

Brazil is the world's largest producer and consumer of industrial charcoal (about 7.3M tonnes in 1992), and one of the few countries that preserved and expanded its charcoal-based iron and steel industry after coke was introduced in other countries. This is partly because the country possesses abundant iron-ore deposits and extensive forest resources, but little coal. Instead of using imported coke, Brazil turned to charcoal as a reduction and thermal agent for use in blast furnaces. It is also unique in modern times because it has improved and developed charcoal technology for use on a large industrial scale.

The charcoal-based pig-iron and steel industry is now at a crossroads. It faces serious socio-economic, environmental, and financial pressures to change and innovate. The industry faces tough challenges ahead – a painful adjustment to falling demand, overcapacity, greater competition with coke, and stricter environmental control of the steel industry in general. The Brazilian steel industry, particularly during the past two decades, was able to expand rapidly because of the combination of increasing demand in both the domestic and export markets. This may not continue in the future.

Despite these difficulties, the charcoal-based pig-iron and steel industry can overcome these challenges and become a modern and thriving industry. Any change in this sector would have enormous socio-economic ramifications, particularly in the State of Minas Gerais. Charcoal has a number of thermal and reduction advantages over coke, not to mention environmental considerations.

The main question now is whether Brazil should continue, or even expand, its production of charcoal on a large scale – a socially and environmentally more acceptable option – or should it use cheap, imported, coke which causes more pollution locally and globally, but may be a cheaper alternative in the short term? The latter is already being considered by various companies. If the charcoal option is chosen, it must include a strong element of 'sustainability', either from plantations or native forests. Thus the charcoal industry has many socio-economic (especially employment) and environmental advantages gains compared with the present system which is destructive and often inefficient. It can even reduce CO_2 emissions, and protect native forests and biodiversity.

Contrary to popular belief, charcoal production and use is increasing worldwide, rather than decreasing. As living standards increase and urbanization occurs, households and cottage industries in many developing countries, especially in Africa, are converting to charcoal. Zambia, for example, has become a major charcoal producer and user only since the late 1960s.

The large-scale use of native or plantation forests causes considerable environmental and ecological concern within both the national and international communities, and Brazil is no exception. These concerns were often justified in the past, although they rarely took into account fully the local socio-economic ramifications. Frequently the concerns were a result of insufficient understanding and knowledge of the local, regional, or even national conditions. In this book we examine these misunderstandings with regard to the charcoal-based industrial sector in Brazil.

Brazil has a long history of charcoal production for iron-making, dating back to the sixteenth century. Then charcoal was produced from the then abundant native forests; more recently it also relies on forest plantations, which currently provide 39 per cent of the total charcoal produced. There are about 2.3 million hectares of plantations for this purpose, mainly eucalyptus, and charcoal is produced on a scale unmatched anywhere else in the world. But it is recognized that unless modern techniques are applied charcoal is, in many ways, a wasteful use of natural resources. Brazilians are learning to modernize quickly in order to survive.

Brazilians are actively involved in the search for new economically and environmentally sustainable means to produce charcoal from plantations and native forests, as is now required by new environmental legislation. 'Sustainable Forest Management Projects' are being carried out, for example, and if proved successful they could set an important precedent in the use and maintenance of large areas of native forests, counteracting the general fear of large-scale deforestation. The importance of these types of projects for preserving native forests should not be overlooked.

Greater environmental control, together with social pressures, means that the charcoal industry will have to change quickly. The same principle applies to the pig-iron sector. For the pig-iron producer or *gusero*, making pig-iron often represents a secondary activity, and as a result the industry suffers from lack of investment and professionalism, although this is now changing.

Imported coke is increasing its share of the charcoal market. For the private sector, mainly concerned with short-term profits, using coke is becoming incréasingly attractive. Already various companies are considering coke as a serious alternative, if only as some kind of 'safety valve' against the potential high cost of charcoal. This represents a major challenge to the charcoal-based industrial sector.

There are many opportunities for the charcoal-based industries to modernize and consolidate. Since coke has long replaced charcoal as the main energy source in industrialized countries, however, there exists a sense of backwardness among some professionals who believe in the inevitability of coke. This attitude contrasts sharply with current trends in many industrialized countries, where biomass sources are increasingly becoming important modern energy carriers. Johansson et al. (1993), for example, have estimated that by the middle of the next century, renewable sources of energy could account for three-fifths of the world's electricity and two-thirds of the market for fuels used directly, of which biomass represents 38 per cent. A 1994/5 study by Shell International Petroleum also predicts a significant role for modernized biomass energy in the next century.

There are important lessons to be learned from the Brazilian experience, including forest management and the industrial production and use of charcoal, and also charcoal's use as a more environmentally friendly and economically viable alternative to coke in thermo-reduction. An important objective of this book is to ensure that this message reaches a much wider audience than Brazil alone. Brazil's experience (poorly known outside the country) is of interest to many other charcoal-producing countries, particularly as an example of natural resource and management use, given its many socio-economic and environmental ramifications.

Most of the expertise and technology is available. What is needed is vision, entrepreneurship, and clear policy to overcome any obstacles that do exist.

A central theme of this book is the need for environmentally and ecologically sustainable production and use of charcoal, either from native forests or commercial plantations. It is argued that the long-term future of the charcoal-based industrial sector in Brazil must be linked to sustainable development.

This book draws a considerable amount of information from extensive field visits to forest plantations, charcoal-making sites, pig-iron and steel plants, personal contact with scientists, foresters, and charcoal-makers, and unpublished literature, in addition to the authors' considerable first-hand experience. Our aim is to present, albeit briefly, a balanced picture of the charcoal-based industrial sector in Brazil.

Chapter 1 is a brief historical description of charcoal in general and Brazil in particular. Brazil's experience with charcoal production dates back to the sixteenth century, although the present modern charcoal-based industrial sector is really just a few decades old.

Chapter 2 briefly examines the pig-iron and steel-based charcoal market and recent developments within this sector; overall pig-iron and steel production and charcoal consumption are analysed.

Chapter 3 deals with charcoal production from native forests and commercial plantations. It examines silvicultural aspects, eucalyptus varieties, plantation densities and methods, seedlings, spacing, cutting age, biodiversity and preservation aspects, insect and weed control, and yields. It also examines a few afforestation programmes in the State of Minas Gerais and the socio-economic aspects of plantations, and ends with some legal aspects of afforestation.

In Chapter 4 we concentrate on the technical and fundamental aspects of charcoal production, charcoal-making technology, and masonry kilns. It also compares the main advantages and disadvantages of charcoal and coke as a thermal and reducing agent in pig-iron and steel making. The chapter also looks at different aspects of charcoal production such as wood density, moisture content, and charcoal density.

Charcoal production costs are discussed in Chapter 5, both from plantations and native forests. Calculating the real costs of charcoal production in Brazil is not an easy matter for a number of reasons. First, costs are site-specific and therefore can vary considerably. Secondly, charcoal prices do not necessarily reflect the real costs, but rather the prevailing market conditions for pig-iron and steel demand. Thirdly, and particularly for charcoal made from native forests by many small producers, charcoal-making is not their main economic activity but is an additional source of income; thus real labour and environmental costs are not fully quantified.

A central theme of this book, the need for environmental and ecological sustainable production and use of charcoal, is taken up in Chapter 6. It examines the possibilities for charcoal production from 'Sustainable Forest Management Projects' (SFMP), particularly in the Carajas region. One such project – Fazenda Descoberta – is analysed in more detail. The Amazon region has an enormous forestry potential which is far from being realized. We argue strongly for the need to find an economic value for the forests as the best guarantee for their survival. SFMP, if successful, can play a vital role in preserving large areas of tropical humid forests in the Amazon; their importance should not be underestimated. The chapter examines different aspects of SFMP which, if conducted wisely, can be the backbone for sustainable development of the region.

The main theme of Chapter 7 is the environment. There is a strong negative perception, rooted in history, about the environmental damage caused by the charcoal-making industry. Charcoal production is associated with various types of environmental problems. The pros and cons are examined in this chapter and compared with those of coke.

Chapter 8 examines the charcoal-based metallurgy sector in general, and some socio-political attitudes. It makes a case for further R&D, particularly with regard to forestry, charcoal production methods, and pig-iron and steel making. It explores the potential use of by-products recovery and the role of potential value-added products in making this sector more competitive.

Finally, Chapter 9 brings together some of the main themes discussed in earlier chapters and draws some conclusions.

Brazil is one of the few countries which preserved and expanded its charcoal-based steel industry after the introduction of coke.

1. Brief History of Charcoal

1.1 General background

It is estimated that about 100M tonnes of charcoal are produced annually worldwide, although this figure may be regarded as a conservative estimate. Charcoal production is an integral part of the informal economy of many developing countries, characterized by small-scale operations involving a large number of small farmers and rural poor people. Charcoal is produced from forestry residues resulting from the expansion of agriculture and pasture land, waste from wood processing, saw mills and forestry's thinnings and, more professionally, from biomass plantations.

In developing countries charcoal is used mainly as a domestic fuel for cooking and heating, but it is also an important industrial and reducing-agent fuel. It is used in numerous metallurgical industries especially pig-iron, foundries, and forges, in cement factories, and for chemical applications. Contrary to popular belief, charcoal consumption has increased in recent years, and is becoming a major source of energy as many people from the rural and urban areas of developing countries convert from wood to charcoal use. When charcoal is destined for metallurgy and other industrial purposes, its quality must be of considerably higher standards and consistency than when it is used for domestic cooking.

The art of charcoal-making is lost in prehistory. In its simplest form, wood is burnt on an open fire and the charred remains are recovered as charcoal. In Egypt, around 3000 BC, a method for embalming and preparing bodies for burial used some of the by-products of charcoal as preserving agents. Some archaeologists have suggested that deforestation resulting from charcoal production may have caused the abandonment of a major iron-making centre around Lake Victoria in central Africa, where people began smelting iron about 2500 years ago (Nooten and Raymaekers, 1988).

In Europe it is known that in about 1000 BC charcoal-making was an important industry for recovering iron and other metals from their ores. Charcoal was the predominant fuel in the iron industry before the Industrial Revolution. Charcoal-based iron-making caused deforestation in England as far back as the 1540s. During the late seventeenth and early eighteenth centuries, the costs and difficulty of obtaining charcoal was a limiting factor in the English iron industry (Ackerman and Almeida, 1990). Indeed, such large tracts of land were deforested in so many parts of the country that by the mid-sixteenth century the deforestation situation became so bad in some areas that a series of enactments intended to

1

preserve the country's woods were issued, particularly aimed at controlling charcoal-based ironworks (Schubert, 1957).

More recently the growing demand for steel in many countries, together with the growing capacity of the chemical industry, brought about an unprecedented demand for charcoal and its liquid by-products. When refined bituminous coal, coke, and lignite became competitive with charcoal, however, the decline of the charcoal industry began. By the time of the First World War many plants were forced to shut down, and although thereafter the industry experienced a revival until the end of the Second World War because of the conflict, the charcoal industry was again hit hard. The development of 'rapid pyrolysis' in late 1950s, one of the most important achievements of charcoal technology, opened up new categories of raw materials such as industrial wastes and agricultural and forestry residues, which were until then untapped (Emrich, 1985).

It is striking, however, that the traditional methods of charcoal-making have changed little from ancient times until the present. As a study by the Food and Agricultural Organization (FAO) illustrates, 'the only new factors are that the simple methodologies have been rationalized and that science has verified the basic processes which take place during carbonization and spelled out the quantitative and qualitative laws which govern the process' (FAO, 1985 p.3). The new methods which have been introduced in some parts of the world have simply supplanted the old technology and the novelty resides only in the rationalization of the use of heat, materials handling, etc., and in some cases the recovery of by-products from the carbonization process (FAO, 1985; Foley, 1986). The survival of this industry must surely be linked to a rapid modernization process and increased efficiency.

A shared characteristic of traditional charcoal-making is low efficiency and many and varied types of techniques, ranging from very simple and cheap earth mouths to the more efficient brick kilns. Commercial charcoal-making, however, often includes sophisticated and expensive technologies such as retorts, which have a high conversion efficiency and are used mainly in industrialized countries.

1.2 Charcoal in Brazil

Brazil is the world's largest producer of charcoal (Table 1.1) and one of the few countries which preserved and expanded its charcoal-based steel industry after the introduction of coke. (Malaysia, Zambia, and the Philippines also use substantial amounts of charcoal for steel-making and other industrial purposes.) This is partly because Brazil possesses abundant iron ore deposits and extensive forest resources, but little coal. Instead of using coke, Brazil used charcoal as a reduction and thermal agent in blast furnaces, well after coke became the dominant source in the industrialized countries. Brazil is also unique in modern times in that it has improved and developed charcoal technology for use on a large industrial scale, although the technology still remains in many ways an art rather than a science. Coke is also widely used in Brazil, representing about 70 per cent of the total heat-reducing agent used.

The origins of charcoal production in the country date back to the late sixteenth century. The first mention of charcoal-based iron works refers to the Sardinha family, who in 1591 were reported to be using charcoal in their foundries to produce iron-ore. The charcoal-based industry has always been heavily concentrated in the state of Minas Gerais (MG), because of the large concentration of iron ore deposits there. It could be said that the history of charcoal production is very much the history of pig-iron and steel production in MG.

It was not until 1812 that a new charcoal-based iron works was reported to be in operation near Congonhas do Campo, State of MG. Between 1813 and 1817 this new pig-iron work used 1000 tonnes of charcoal to produce about 80 tonnes of pig-iron, a conversion rate of 13.7kg of charcoal per kilo of pig-iron (Osse, 1982).

By the early 1880s, more than 80 iron works were reported to be in operation in MG. A study on the 'Mineral Production of the Province of Minas Gerais' stated that in the region between Ouro Preto and Diamantina alone there were at least 80 iron works in operation at that time.

Studies conducted in MG in 1881 and 1883 also indicate that the charcoal production methods were regarded as 'barbarous', particularly when they referred to a very inefficient production method called 'cave' (a method similar to the traditional pit kiln) which, in addition to being inefficient, produced a very poor quality charcoal. The cave consisted of a hole in the ground, between two to three metres in diameter and 0.8m in depth, that was filled up with chipped wood and then covered with a layer of soil, leaving only one outlet, which was also closed once the wood was ignited. This was a very wasteful method of producing charcoal and resulted in the destruction of large areas of native forests. As it was then reported, 'whole forests were being destroyed by this system while a more rational method would have provided wood to produce charcoal for centuries to come' (Sena, 1881; Bovet, 1883; Osse, 1982).

During those first three centuries there seems to have been little charcoal-related industrial activity in Brazil, and the charcoal-based iron industry remained very small, almost an artisan activity. From the 1890s to the 1930s, however, some significant advances were reported to have been made, such as the introduction of more advanced and more efficient kilns.

During the First World War, and then again from the 1930s, new steel-making plants were built, many of them charcoal-based. In the 1970s, the industry appears to have reached some kind of maturity, and was officially recognized among politicians and industrialists, for the first time, as 'the only proven technological and economically viable alternative . . . as an independent energy source, whose development should form the basic pillar of Brazil's steel industry' (Instituto Brasileiro de Siderurgia, 1980; Osse, 1982).

Studies published during the 1970s showed that during the previous few decades, the charcoal-based iron and steel industry consisted of a great diversity of kilns with varying capacities, degrees of efficiency, mechanization, equipment, operating systems, type, and and quality of products. Since the 1970s and the worldwide oil price increases, the charcoal-based pig-iron and steel industries underwent considerable expansion as a result of the oil import substitution programmes initiated by successive Brazilian governments.

In the 1980s, a major objective of the industry through the programme of 'rationalization of charcoal use and improvement of productivity for the non-integrated steel mills', was to reduce the volumetric conversion of charcoal-to-pig-iron from about 0.92 tonnes per tonne in 1978 to 0.85 tonnes per tonne in 1983. A major new development was the creation of a pig-iron and steel complex in the Carajas region of the Amazon.

From 1990 until the end of 1993, the economic crisis that affected Brazil, in particular, resulted in a sharp decrease in demand in steel production, especially pig-iron. This, together with new legislation aimed at protecting native forests, forced the sector to re-examine its long-term future and to search for new alternatives, such as diversification and cost cutting.

The history of charcoal production and use in Brazil can be briefly summarized as follows:

(a) 1591 to 1812. This includes the period between the registration of the first and second charcoal foundry. The main characteristic was the very low efficiency of charcoal production and use in iron works. Little concern was shown for the then abundant raw material (native forests), either by farmers, livestock ranchers, or charcoal producers. Total charcoal and pig-iron production was, however, very small, and remained almost an artisan activity.

(b) 1814 to the late nineteenth century. During this period various types of foundries were operating, with greater efficiency and more specialized uses. It was during this period that the first serious criticism appeared about the irrational destruction of the native forests resulting from the activities of farmers, cattle ranchers, and charcoal-makers; calls were made for greater production efficiency and control, and for the preservation of the forests.

(c) Late nineteenth century to 1930s. This period was characterized by some improvements in charcoal-making techniques, including better operating methods and the introduction of more advanced blast furnaces, but few advances of any significance were made and no important measures were taken to preserve the forests, either for charcoal-making or any other purposes.

(d) 1930s to 1970s. The first studies of charcoal production and consumption by the charcoal-based industry appeared were carried out during the

4

1930s. These studies considered the new improvements, the rationalization of the pig-iron and steel sector, increased productivity, and greater concern for native forests. During the 1940s the iron and steel industry finally adopted a policy of 'afforestation' as the best and cheapest way to guarantee the supply of raw material to produce charcoal. This resulted in a rapid expansion of afforestation activities, particularly with eucalyptus. These developments were further stimulated by the increase in oil prices in the early 1970s, which resulted in a rapid expansion of the charcoal industry.

(e) 1980 to early 1990s. The main development and expansion of the charcoal-based iron works began in the mid-1980s in the Carajas region, in the Eastern part of the Amazon. The Carajas Project differed considerably from other developments in Brazil in at least two respects: (i) it was an opportunity to take a more modern approach to charcoal production and use; and (ii) the region lacked experience in charcoal-making, which had to be transferred mainly from MG. Some experts, however, compared the charcoal industry in Carajas to that of MG during the 1950s from which little progress has been made.

(f) From 1990. Some industrialists and professionals in the industry began to worry about the high cost of charcoal and the possible supply problems, and expressed doubts about the long-term future of the industry.

Overall, despite Brazil's long tradition and historical experience in charcoal-making, the present industry should be considered a young one, since all the leading companies in this sector have been working with charcoal on an industrial scale only during the past few decades.

2. The Charcoal-based Industrial Sector

There have been four main expansion phases, all of which occurred in the twentieth century (Assis et al., 1982).

(a) 1924 to 1946. Annual production of steel increased from 4500 tonnes to 342 000 tonnes (an average annual increase of 22 per cent), with charcoal as the main source of energy.

(b) 1946 to 1960. Production increased to about 1.9M tonnes per year. A major characteristic was the diversification of products, and the introduction of imported coke on a significant scale for use in the industry.

(c) 1960 to 1964. Steel production reached 3M tonnes, an annual growth of 12 per cent, with two major new steel-making companies, USIMINAS and COSIPAR, starting production.

(d) 1964 to 1980. This period is characterized by a rapid production increase, from about 3 to 15.4M tonnes annually, with an average increase of 8.5 per cent per year. The major feature of this period was the increased use of imported coke at the expense of charcoal, whose percentage use fell from 70 per cent in 1940 to 36 per cent in 1980.

(e) 1980 onwards. The main feature was the creation of a new charcoal-based pig-iron and steel centre in the Carajas region, which currently represents 3.5 per cent of Brazil's total pig-iron production.

2.1 Main features of the iron and steel industry

The steel industry can be divided into five main groups (ABRACAVE, 1992):

o coke-based integrated steel plants
o charcoal-based integrated steel plants
o semi-integrated charcoal-based steel plants
o independent pig-iron plants
o ferro-alloys plants

Table 2.1 summarizes pig-iron and steel production according to the main consuming sectors.

Coke-based integrated steel plants. These plants use iron ore and coal. Steel is produced in five main technical steps: a coke-oven battery, a sinterization process, a blast furnace, a steel-making converter, and iron casting. This is a conventional way of producing steel on a large scale, so it works well in large steel plants. Within this group there are five companies, each with a capacity of between two and four million tonnes per year. In 1992 these plants produced nearly 16M tonnes, or about 70 per cent of the 22.6M tonnes total steel production. They consumed about eight million tonnes of coke, almost 100 per cent from imported coal.

Charcoal-based integrated steel plants. In 1992 these plants produced about 4.3M tonnes of steel, about 19 per cent of the total in small- to medium-scale plants of 0.4 to 0.9M tonnes per year. There are nine companies operating, and they usually purchase charcoal from third parties but also purchase from their own plantations. Charcoal and ore is fed into small blast furnaces that convert the material into pig-iron using a steel-making converter. Steel is produced in its final form by a series of casting equipment.

Non- and semi-integrated steel plants. These plants buy scrap metal and pig-iron from independent producers. A blast furnace is used for smelting and refining the raw material from which casting steel is obtained. There are about 20 companies in this group, with the most common capacities being between 0.15 and 0.30M tonnes per year, although some of the smaller plants have capacities of less than 10 000 tonnes per year. Total production in 1992 was about 2.5M tonnes of steel – 11 per cent of the total.

Independent pig-iron plants. These plants produce only pig iron and are much simpler, using small charcoal-based blast furnaces. There are about 78 companies, and their capacity varies from 60 000 to 300 000 tonnes per year. These plants produced 4.5M tonnes, and consumed about 3.75M tonnes of charcoal. The pig-iron is sold to non-integrated steel industries and is also exported. This industry has historically been (and still is) concentrated in the State of MG.

Ferro-alloys plants. This sector has 24 companies in operation, with 115 kilns and a production of about 1M tonnes of ferro-alloys in 1992. This sector is very dependent on charcoal, which provides 98 per cent of the energy of the industry, with a total consumption of about 0.7M tonnes in 1992.

An independent pig-iron plant is usually inefficient since, for example, it cannot use excess blast-furnace gas. In comparison an integrated steel plant, which has other kilns for steel processing, has a much higher energy efficiency. An additional advantage is that these plants can generate higher value products like steel pipes, stainless steel, etc. In the long term, the future of the charcoal-based steel and other related sectors will probably be very much linked to integrated steel-processing plants.

2.2 Overall charcoal consumption in the pig-iron and other industrial sectors

About 7.3M tonnes of charcoal were produced in Brazil in 1992, (61 per cent from native forests and 39 per cent from biomass plantations – see Table 1.1), compared with about 11.2M tonnes in the peak year of 1989. The State of MG consumed about 80 per cent of the charcoal, approximately 5.8M tonnes in 1992, followed by the Carajas region with 0.85M tonnes, and the state of Bahia with about 0.25M tonnes. Thus native forests continue to provide the majority of the charcoal, although there has been a steady decline (with minor fluctuations) since the 1970s from about 88 per cent in 1978 to about 61 per cent in 1992 (ABRACAVE, 1993).

With the large-scale plantations developed over the last 20 years, one would have expected more charcoal to have been produced from them. A number of reasons are suggested to explain the discrepancy. First, charcoal consumers still find it cheaper to produce or buy charcoal from native forests, despite high transport costs (distances of over 1000km are common), because the wood is obtained free or at a low cost. Unlike plantations, this type of charcoal-making tends to be a marginal activity in most cases, with the small producer paying hardly any taxes. According to Neto (1993), if such illegal activities were curtailed and all taxes paid, and if charcoal was to be produced professionally, charcoal from native forests would be as costly as that produced from plantations. Large amounts of charcoal also continue to be made from waste trees resulting from the expansion of agriculture and pasture land, again avoiding the costs associated with forestry plantations. Secondly, wood from plantations fetches higher prices when sold for other industrial uses like pulp and paper, cellulose, and furniture, than when sold for charcoal. Recent legislation is changing this, as will be explained later. Thirdly, charcoal is, to a large extent, produced mainly for pig-iron producers by many small independent individuals who do not own plantations or have the necessary resources to do so. Fourthly, the contribution from eucalyptus plantations has been lower than expected because of the low productivity of first trials on poor quality land. This situation is already changing because of the continuous advances in productivity.

The amount of charcoal produced from native forests in absolute terms has declined sharply in the last few years, from about 8M tonnes in 1989 to 4.4M tonnes in 1992. At the same time charcoal from plantations has risen slightly in percentage terms, while decling in absolute terms from about 3.2M tonnes to about 2.8M tonnes in the same period. The decline in charcoal from native forests can be attributed to factors such as tougher environmental law enforcement, lower demand for pig-iron in the early 1990s, and high transportation costs. It is expected that charcoal production from plantations, chiefly of eucalyptus, will continue to increase both in absolute and relative terms in the coming years. The degree of such growth will be determined by the price of charcoal, the extent and success of the industrial restructuring and the level of substitution by coke, which in turn will also be partly determined by the price of charcoal.

The charcoal-based pig-iron industry has also been declining in recent years because of a combination of factors such as fluctuating market conditions, new changes after the privatization of various large companies, competition from coke, perceived supply problems, lack of professionalism and unreliability of small charcoal-producers, and high transport costs. According to ABIFA (Associacao Brasileira das Industrias de Fundicao), however, the market for the pig-iron sector is expected to grow again in the near future and the actual capacity may have to be more than doubled to meet domestic and export demand by the year 2000 (Grupo Itaminas, 1991). This prediction seems too optimistic given present market conditions, the relatively high cost of charcoal, possible competition from coke in certain areas, and the high investment costs that this industry will require in order to modernize. Other studies, however, also indicate that the market for pig-iron will expand in the future (CVRD, 1992).

Most of the smaller pig-iron mills are still very inefficient. Traditionally, for many small pig-iron producers, such production only represents an additional income and thus they have shown little interest in re-investing in the sector. The consequence is that this industry is undercapitalized and lacks the necessary professionalism and innovative drive. Unless important cultural changes occur, this sector will find it difficult to survive in its present form in the medium to long term.

Table 2.2 shows charcoal consumption in the main industrial sectors in Brazil from 1988 to 1992. The total consumption of charcoal in all industrial sectors fell from the 1989 peak of 11.2M tonnes to 7.3M tonnes in 1992. Of this 7.3M, 6.2M tonnes were used by the steel-related sectors, with the state of MG representing nearly 79 per cent of the total, and 0.3M tonnes were used by the cement-related sectors.

Charcoal's other important industrial applications in Brazil include food and drinks, ceramics, pulp and paper, textiles, and chemicals. Brazil also exports charcoal, mainly to North America and Europe. During the period of 1980–91 about 148 000 tonnes, worth over US$13.5M, were exported (ABRACAVE, 1991; ABRACAVE, 1993).

3. Raw Material for Charcoal Production: From Native Forests to Forest Plantations

An important historical feature of charcoal production in Brazil is that a large part of the raw material has come from deforestation as a result of the expansion of agriculture and cattle ranching. Until recently, forests were seen as an obstacle with little or no economic value; something to be disposed of, often burnt to make way for agriculture and animal grazing. When forests were abundant, there was little concern shown by either the government, farmers, or the pig-iron foundries to protect or preserve them. As far back as 1894 the *Industrial Journal of MG* wrote 'the barbarous method of setting fire to the forests, already used in the previous century to facilitate the exploration of mineral deposits – and still being used today for agricultural land clearing – has had the serious consequence of deforesting large areas, making it very difficult to produce charcoal near the iron-ore mines' (Osse, 1982).

As pig-iron production continued to expand, and forests were progressively being cut, it became apparent to the industry that a rational and sustainable exploitation of native forests was essential for their survival. Thus the theory of 'natural afforestation', as it was then called, gained ground during the nineteenth century: native forest, if allowed, would regenerate spontaneously by using cheap and simple management techniques. This idea was well received by the charcoal-based iron industry, and as a result a significant number of companies started to preserve and expand native forests under their own control.

This did not result in sustainable forestry, partly because the forests were cut too frequently, and partly because of the lack of technical and scientific support. The idea of 'natural afforestation' was therefore finally abandoned in the 1940s, when it was thought inadequate to supply sufficient charcoal to the expanding steel industry. Afforestation, then meaning eucalyptus plantations, was thought the best guarantee of a sufficient and cheap supply of charcoal. As Navarro Andrade noted: '. . . without charcoal there will not be pig-iron and without eucalyptus there will not be charcoal . . .' (Andrade, 1961; Osse, 1982).

3.1 History of forest plantations

Forest plantations are nothing new. People have been planting trees for thousands of years for food and shelter, and for ceremonial, religious, and other purposes. The present development of plantations can be traced back to the sixteenth and seventeenth centuries when exploration and expansion of European influence took place. Prior to 1900 there was no need to plant trees on a large scale as an industrial resource though there was some concern, particularly in some European countries, about their lack of natural forests (Evans, 1992).

The period from 1900 to 1945 saw the first extensive plantings of industrial tree crops, mostly in countries with little useable natural forest. In the period between 1945 and 1965 plantation forestry was influenced by a number of additional factors, including internationalism and awareness of silvicultural potential. The period from the mid-1960s to 1980 saw the acceleration of the trends initiated in the previous period; new projects multiplied, and afforestation became an important part of many national forest policies. Using data from FAO, Evans (1992) has estimated the extent of plantations established in the tropics at 11.5Mha in 1980: 7.2Mha for industrial and 4.3Mha for non-industrial purposes.

Several new silvicultural trends began to take shape in the 1980s – agroforestry and social forestry. Tree planting is no longer only for industrial purposes; its uses range from fuelwood, timber, and industrial wood to environmental control. Plantation establishment rates accelerated in the late 1970s. Evans (1993) has estimated the net forest plantation areas in the tropics (90 countries), at 43.8Mha. In 1992 industrial plantations accounted for 15.6Mha and non-industrial for 28.2Mha.

In Brazil, the first we hear of afforestation is the city of Rio de Janeiro, where it was reported in 1860 that some 120 000 seedlings of native tree species were planted on the hills of Morro de Tijuca. Commercial afforestation did not actually commence until early this century with the introduction of eucalyptus species. During the late 1940s and early 1950s, other species were also introduced, particularly pines. In 1948 the Companhia Belgo-Mineira was the first private company to opt for eucalyptus plantations to produce charcoal. The company owned some 90 000ha in MG, while Acesita Forestal had about 40 000ha (Osse, 1982). By 1950 the Federal Forestry Service was reported to be very pleased with the progress made by the charcoal-making sector in substituting native forest for eucalyptus as its raw material.

There was increasing concern about the fate of native forests and the potentially acute supply problems. During a meeting of the steel industry of the states of MG and Sao Paulo in October 1951 this concern became apparent. It was then forecast that MG would exhaust its native forest by 1972, if trends continued unabated. This prediction did not materialize as it underestimated the capacity of the *cerrado* to regenerate.

During the 1950s the industry appears to have opted for afforestation on a much larger scale, judging by the number of companies that were (or planned to be) involved in this activity. The estimated planted area in the mid-1950s was about 0.5Mha. With the enactment of the Forestry Code in 1965 and the Fiscal Incentive Law in 1966, planting gained even more

11

impetus. By 1970 some five hundred different companies were reported to be involved in various afforestation activities. Average annual planting rose to about 0.4Mha during the 1974–82 period (Pandey, 1992). (See Table 3.1). Decree Law 1376 of 1974 further stimulated the afforestation process and gave, for the first time, priority to charcoal production. In 1974, Decree Law 79046 also regulated fiscal incentives for the charcoal industry. Fiscal incentives for afforestation were finally abolished in December 1987. This resulted in a considerable decline in planting activities. In 1992 the area being planted in the whole country was estimated to be only about 100 000ha per year (Neto, personal communication and 1993; Caixeta and Braga, 1993). Furtado (personal communication), however, estimates plantation establishment of 150 000ha per year and Pandey (1992) calculates 200 000ha per year.

In addition to increased timber supply through fiscal incentives, the government had several other important objectives, such as to diversify the rural economy and generate employment in the rural milieu, to attract foreign investment, and to conserve the forest.

It is difficult to provide comprehensive figures on afforestation in Brazil given the fragmentary (and often conflicting) nature of the data available. Ferreira (1989) quotes a total plantation area of 5.2Mha in 1983 (about 1.6Mha of pines, 2.8Mha of eucalypts, and 0.8Mha of others), and Rodriguez (1991) calculated a reforested area of 0.5Mha in 1964 and 5.8Mha in 1987. Jesus (1990) reported a higher estimate of about 6.2Mha in 1988 (52 per cent eucalypts, 30 per cent pines, and 18 per cent other species). Pandey (1992) estimated the planted area in 1990 to be 6.1Mha. The planted area for Minas Gerais was estimated at about 2Mha in 1992, and consisted mostly of eucalypts for charcoal production (Furtado, personal communication).

There are many reasons for these discrepancies: much of the data may be based on an initially planted (or planned) area without taking into account fully the death rate (which can be high, depending on the climatic and soil conditions); and many projects were never fully implemented, were planted with the wrong species, or were simply abandoned in the first two years. There was also duplication of planted areas, inadequate protection and aftercare because of a lack of finance, and incorrect reporting.

About 90 per cent of the plantations established in Brazil up until 1987 were owned by large private companies and wealthy individuals. Approximately 40 per cent of the plantations were established to provide raw material for the pulp and paper industry; 25 per cent for plywood and particleboard, etc.; and 35 per cent to produce charcoal for smelting pig-iron (Pandey, 1992).

The success of afforestation in Brazil can be attributed to a combination of factors. These were favourable conditions which contributed to high productivity, such as the availability of cheap land, abundant and low-cost labour in the rural areas, and historical experience. Important fiscal incentives were also introduced in the 1960s. The fiscal incentives allowed Brazil-based companies to deduct over 25 per cent of their tax bills if the money was spent on afforestation projects approved by the Instituto Brasileiro de Desenvolvimento Florestal (IBDF). The incentives included all costs involved in establishing an afforestation project, excluding land.

In 1974 the government launched the National Cellulose and Paper Programme, whose aim was to achieve self-sufficiency in pulp and paper and enable the export of 2M tonnes in 1980 and 20M tonnes in 2000. This programme has been quite successful. In 1992 the production of pulp and paper reached 4.9M tonnes, and cellulose almost 4.9M tonnes. About 1.23M tonnes and 1.64M tonnes of the products were exported, worth $1.47 billion. This industry represents about 1.2 per cent of Brazil's GNP (approximately $5.1 billion), employs directly over 121 000 people, and owns 1.4Mha of plantations. The industry invested $5.5 billion from 1989 to 1992 and has a further $4.7 billion earmarked for new projects (ANFPC, 1993).

Another programme which has further stimulated afforestation activities was the National Steel Development Programme, which also originated from the Government's desire to make Brazil a major exporter of steel products. The combination of these circumstances, together with the expansion of charcoal production, played a key role in the expansion of afforestation activities.

3.2 Silvicultural aspects

Brazil has the world's largest forest reserves. Its land area is 851Mha, of which about 670Mha are covered by natural forests of some description, including 300Mha of broadleaves (Rodriguez, 1991).

The first pioneering work with intensive silviculture was initiated by Armando Navarro de Andrade of the Companhia Paulista de Estradas de Ferros in 1904. The basic philosophy of intensive silviculture was to produce the greatest possible amount of wood, for a given unit area, in the shortest possible time and in the most economical way possible. Although it was accepted that native forests were more adapted to their environment, it was also recognized that they were not necessarily the most productive species. Navarro de Andrade demonstrated in Brazil that new species such as eucalyptus could be far more productive than the local native trees (Ferreira, 1989).

Because of their very good growth characteristics, climatic adaptability, and wide-ranging usefulness, eucalypts soon became one of the most important and most widely planted trees. This was true not only in Brazil but also around the world. There are about 10Mha in 90 tropical countries alone (Evans, 1993). The genus eucalyptus was first described and named by L'Heritier in 1788, and about 600 species and nearly 140 varieties are known today.

3.3 Eucalyptus varieties and wood densities

Eucalyptus was soon accepted in Brazil because of its adaptability to the country's conditions. At the beginning of commercial plantations only a few species were planted, such as *E.grandis* and *E.saligna*, because of both their previous success and the availability of seeds from South Africa. Those species gave good results in the state of Sao Paulo and later in Minas Gerais and Espirito Santo, always in good soil and with abundant rainfall. The first plantations were destined for pulp and paper production.

When large afforestation schemes for charcoal production began, these two species were also planted in drier regions with poorer soils, without first being properly tested, in the expectation that they would repeat past good results especially in terms of fast growth rate. These expectations were not fulfilled, however, and the species failed to adapt readily to the poorer conditions. An additional problem was that some varieties have low wood densities, which results in lower charcoal quality.

The pig-iron and metallurgical-based charcoal industries were accustomed to working with high wood densities from native forest charcoal (*cerrado* is 250kg/m^3), and were not content to work with lower charcoal densities. Measurements carried out by Acesita in 1985 at Itamarandiba, MG, found densities of eucalyptus charcoal as low as 170 and 200kg/m^3 (Furtado, personal communication).

In the early 1980s new species were introduced, mainly *E. camaldulensis, E. urophylla, E. cloesiana, E. citriodora* and other varieties which seem to adapt better to poorer soil and shorter rain periods and with the additional advantage of having a higher wood and charcoal density.

A considerable effort has been made by the large steel companies like Acesita, Belgo-Mineira, Mannesmann, and Pains together with the main Forestry Research Institutes of the country, to import high quality eucalyptus seeds, particularly from Australia. This has been done to select those varieties suitable for charcoal production. Today most of the Brazilian eucalyptus hybrids originate from Australia, South Africa, New Zealand, and Timor Island in Indonesia. The majority of young seedlings are grown from seed which has been selected to meet specific local or regional conditions (Macedo, personal communication).

The average wood density today is around 230kg/m^3 (eucalyptus), and about 250kg/m^3 for native forest from the *cerrado* region. The plans are to achieve values of around 270kg/m^3. In the Carajas region, the charcoal density is between 270 and 280kg/m^3, and the ratio of charcoal to pig-iron is 2.6m^3 (about 650kg) of charcoal per tonne of pig-iron. This high efficiency is also partly a result of better and newer kilns in that region (Furtado, 1993).

3.4 Seedling generation and planting methods

A considerable effort has been made by the major plantations, including the pig-iron smelting and steel companies, to generate good seedlings from the selected varieties. Most of the larger companies have their own ongoing tree improvement management programmes. On a commercial basis most companies are now using vegetative root propagation techniques or root cuttings. The cuttings are grown in dibble tubes in a vermiculite and bark mixture. The nursery process normally involves 35 to 40 days in a shade house, then the trees are moved outside for another 35 to 40 days.

Planting methods vary widely amongst the companies. Acesita, for example, prefers to plant hybrids and to generate their seedlings by vegetative growth of leaf cuttings, which are planted manually. Other companies, such as Mannesmann, have opted to use vegetative growth only to select trees and generate seed matrices. Mannesmann generally grows the seedlings from seed, rather than from coppices, and the company claims that this generates a material more resistant to lower rainfall after planting, and is also more suitable for mechanized planting. Coppicing is also widely used in Brazil, but yields are reported to be about 20 per cent lower on average. As much as 60 per cent decline in productivity has also been reported in some cases after the first coppicing. Only in good soil and climatic conditions can productivity usually be maintained, or even improved, compared with the first coppicing (Macedo, personal communication).

Coppice plantations are often fertilized. Phosphate and lime are usually applied because of the acidic nature of the soils. Each individual tree is fertilized at planting with about 150g of nitrogen and 200g of superphosphate, and in addition trace elements of baron and zinc are also applied. Fertilization is not used again until the coppice is harvested, when about 500kg/ha may be added, but this is not always the case. Coppice plantations for charcoal are not normally fertilized, partly because the lower productivity and large number of small branches and residues left in the ground after the first cut makes this task more difficult.

3.5 Tree spacing and cutting age

Evidence so far indicates that there is a strong relationship between tree-spacing and final volume: the wider the spacing the greater the volume. This is only true up to a certain level, however, since if the spacing is too wide the plantation becomes uneconomic.

Early eucalyptus plantations in Brazil have had a traditional spacing of 3 × 3m, but in the 1970s a common concept in the charcoal-oriented

15

plantations was the so-called 'energy forest', which uses smaller spacing between the tree rows and young cuttings. The distance within and between rows reached the extreme of 1 × 1.5m (approximately 5000 trees per ha) and a cutting age of four years, a practice initiated in the state of MG. With the expansion of the planted area, new methods were tried to select new varieties more suitable to local conditions and end-use as pulp and paper, charcoal, and timber.

Current trends are to use wider spacings to facilitate harvesting and weed control and to reduce wind damage, as well as for intercropping purposes. For example, Mannesmann uses 3 × 3m to allow mechanized planting to reduce plantation costs, while Acesita uses a different arrangement, with varying distances in the rows (such as 4, 3, 3, 3, 4m) and constant distance between the rows. The spacing between rows varies with region, but it is usually as follows: low rainfall: 1.5m; medium rainfall: 2.0m; good soil with good rainfall: 2.5m.

If charcoal is the intended end use, however, higher planting densities may be preferable. Densities of about 2200 trees per hectare with three coppices and a six-year cycle have been found best from a present net value standpoint (Betters et al., 1992), compared to the 5000 trees per hectare preferred in the 1970s.

In the case of the cutting cycle, the tendency today is to use seven years for all cycles. If the wood is intended for pulp and paper, only wood with a minimum diameter of 6cm is used, compared to 3cm in the case of charcoal. The present trend is to generate bigger trees to reduce forest disturbance (for environmental considerations) and also to cut harvesting costs which are responsible for about half of the delivered cost of wood. It is also accepted nowadays that the highest growth rate occurs during the fourth and fifth years after a good root system is established. In this way a much higher return is obtained on the investment than would otherwise be the case.

With wider spacing, intercropping is possible. Small-scale plantations are being intercropped with crops such as maize and beans during the first year(s) to offset establishment costs. Experiments are also being carried out with grazing animals, particularly cows, by the Mannesmann Group. Grass can grow easily under eucalyptus trees, and it is expected that 2ha will be able to sustain at least one cow for long periods. This is of particular interest in areas where weed control may be necessary in order to protect the plantations. Grazing should be allowed only after the second year of planting, however, to avoid damage to young trees. Overgrazing should also be avoided as this could cause soil erosion and lower plantation yields.

3.6 Biodiversity preservation and insect control

New environmental laws on plantations in Brazil require that 30 per cent of the natural vegetation must be left untouched, in particular the *veredas* (valleys between the flat hills, which are also frequently wetter). In early eucalyptus plantations some companies planted large areas, leaving only a few isolated and often inaccessible areas for native forests to grow in. A consensus is now emerging, particularly among the more professionally advanced companies, that such an approach is an ineffective way of controlling pests and diseases and can result in heavy losses from caterpillars unless large amounts of insecticides are used. Thus it makes economic sense to plant less land rather than the whole area in order to encourage biological pest control.

It is also generally accepted that the preservation areas should be left in the middle of the planted forests, and interconnected with some type of strip to enhance natural pest control and encourage biodiversity. Acesita, for example, with a 140 000ha eucalyptus plantation, has been experimenting with a net of strips 250m wide and 5km apart from one another, where natural vegetation has been allowed to regrow. Acesita Forestal (a sister-company of Acesita) no longer uses insecticides for insect control, except for leaf-cutting ants. Different species and varieties of eucalyptus planted in blocks were used to minimize insect attacks which, when they occur, are allowed to run their course.

In the plantations of the Mannesmann Group, the strips connecting the preservation areas are 25m wide by 400m. Research to establish the flight distances for small birds to help to control caterpillars led to these narrower planted spaces. Mannesmann also uses biological control (predator insects), and some insecticides for pest and disease control.

Weed control is very important, especially during the first two years. In Brazil, weeding is normally done every six months, often manually. Larger companies may use tractors to disk between rows. Herbicides are also used before planting.

Leaf-cutting ants, particularly of the genera *Atta* and *Acromyrmex*, are one of the major enemies of forest plantations in Brazil as they can cause serious damage to plantations if not properly controlled. Insecticide is usually applied to the soil to combat them.

3.7 Yields

The productivity of eucalypt and pine plantations in Brazil varies widely, ranging from 4t/ha/yr in poorer dry soil to as high as 35t/ha/yr (trial plots), with the national average ranging from 10 to 12.5t/ha/yr. Good commercial plantations in MG produce about 17t/ha/yr. There is the potential to achieve 20 to 28t/ha/yr in many areas (Ferreira, personal communication). In these instances there is a long-term commitment to research and monitoring for optimum productivity, well-trained personnel, and long-term planning. It also frequently incorporates environmental practices which ensure biodiversity and minimal chemical inputs. During the last decade the harvestable area in MG was about 1.4Mha of eucalyptus, approximately 140 000ha planted annually, (with an average of about 1300 trees per hectare and a standing biomass of 42 tonnes per hectare). The harvested area of pine during the same period was about 103 000ha, approximately 10 300ha annually (about 1800 trees per hectare and average green matter of 66 tonnes per hectare) (IBAMA/MG, 1991).

A major problem in the early 1980s was the lack of good quality and quantities of seeds and seedlings, particularly in the case of eucalyptus. This problem has been largely overcome and today Brazil can supply good quality seeds and seedlings from cuttings to plant over 0.5Mha annually. Other aspects which have been significantly improved are the use of vegetatively sprouted cuttings with a very high survival rate, and the genetic selection of eucalypts. The overall survival rate of biomass plantations in Brazil has increased quite significantly – from about 70 per cent in the 1960s to nearly 90 per cent in the 1980s (Pandey, 1992; Rivelli and Rezende, 1989).

3.8 Afforestation programmes for charcoal production in Minas Gerais

A major afforestation programme called FLOREMINAS (Polo Florestal Minas Gerais) is currently being implemented in MG. The objective of this programme is to plant approximately 3Mha in a 10-year period, mainly for charcoal production, in an area of about 210 000km^2 around the steel production region of this state. The aim is to release pressure on native forests and meet federal law requirements towards achieving sustainable production of charcoal.

All the major sites in the state of MG were surveyed and this showed that about 5.4Mha was available for afforestation, including old inefficient eucalyptus plantations, degraded pastures, and deforested areas. The plan foresees the management and planting of 300 000ha per year which will include: 20 000ha/year of natural forests to be managed on a sustainable basis; 80 000ha/year of old eucalyptus plantations for replanting; 150 000ha/year of commercial plantations decreasing gradually each year; and 50 000ha/year increased gradually to over 100 000ha/year to be planted in small-scale forestry designated projects.

This programme is being put together by ABRACAVE, SINDIFER and other private companies, in collaboration with the government of the state of MG and federal and international agencies, and aims to raise the necessary funding.

The programme will include the introduction of the best and most modern environmental techniques in accordance with new environmental legislation to include keeping a minimum of 30 per cent of the areas in natural reserves, preserving biodiversity, protecting water, and planting fruits and native trees in some critically depleted areas to enhance bird and insect life. 'FLOREMINAS does not aim to maximize productivity. It aims to reconcile socio-economic interests; to diversify the different components capable of revolutionizing this sector through a realistic and simplified model' (ABRACAVE, 1993a). Because of a combination of factors such as a lack of funding and fiscal incentives, recession, etc., this programme is running behind schedule and, as things stand at the moment, is unlikely to reach its intended objectives, at least in the short term.

There is another small-scale farm forestry scheme called 'Programa Fazendeiro Florestal' (PPF), which receives support from the charcoal producers. The project aims to assist small farmers who want to use part of their land to plant eucalyptus, usually in areas of poor soil quality which tend to be unsuitable for agriculture. Alternative schemes began to be devised in the early 1960s which aimed to support the small farmer, to improve socio-economic conditions, and also to guarantee the supply of raw material (wood, charcoal, etc.) to the local markets. These programmes are particularly attractive for the large charcoal consumers after government subsidies for afforestation were withdrawn in the late 1980s. This type of scheme represents a low-cost afforestation strategy both in economic and financial terms and avoids the need to purchase additional land, or to spend on new infrastructure and labour costs. It can also improve the use of local land and labour resources.

For this reason the programme 'Fazendeiro Florestal' appears to have considerable potential for success. According to Neto (personal communication) charcoal costs represent an investment of between $200 and $300 per hectare to the large charcoal consumers, and very little for the small farmer. For the small farmer charcoal production is normally an additional activity requiring only his land (usually of little agricultural value) and his labour which he gives in his spare time.

The PFF scheme appears to have already brought various socio-economic benefits to the local small farmer because: (a) it allowed the incorporation of new land into a productive system which was previously of little value; (b) it resulted in financial gains for the small farmers; and (c) it reduced the pressure (albeit on a small scale) on the native forests. Altogether over 51 000ha had been reforested under such schemes by 1992 with varying degrees of success (see Table 3.2).

Current plans to stimulate small-scale forestry are quite ambitious and will probably have to rely on private companies which have considerable experience with afforestation. Such plans also need logistical support from the state government as a guarantor of loans. The plans, as shown above, will begin with 50 000ha/year, gradually increasing to more than 100 000ha/year.

3.9 Socio-economic factors

The charcoal industry has historically had a poor, if not negative, image because rightly or wrongly, it has often been associated with poor working conditions, environmental damage, deforestation, backwardness, massive eucalyptus plantations, etc. In addition, large eucalyptus plantations have also been associated in some areas with loss of agricultural land, soil erosion, and environmental degradation.

This image is beginning to change thanks to a better understanding of the industry by the general public, efforts to improve it, and greater environmental and social awareness. The industry is looking for alternatives in favour of 'sustainable development' and is already actively involved in environmental and conservation programmes of various types. There are still many instances, however, in which charcoal production is associated with destructive practices, if one excludes charcoal from plantations.

Contrary to popular believe, many plantations have been set up in areas of low population density and poor and under-used land. This has stimulated development and increased employment in rural areas. A recent study by Abrahao and Furtado (1992), for example shows that in areas where large plantations have been established, there have been positive socio-economic effects on the local population. The study covers the 'Alto Jequitinhonha' valley, an area with a heavy concentration of plantations, many of which are owned by Acesita. Before 1974, when the afforestation started, emigration from this area was high. This situation was reversed when plantation activities started, with the creation of new employment opportunities which have largely been maintained over the years. Agricultural production also increased, contrary to what is often assumed. In general, in areas where there have been large reforestation activities, the living standard of the local population is much higher than in villages where this activity did not take place. According to Abrahao and Furtado (1992), 'The reforestation activities promoted and stimulated the socio-economic conditions of the region. It created employment, particularly in the rural sector, generated capital formation, increased local taxes, stopped migration, increased food production . . . and improved socio-economic development in general.'

The charcoal-based sector directly employed over 180 000 people in 1992, down from 268 000 in 1989 (see Table 3.3). Afforestation is labour intensive – about 5ha/yr per person – and the costs per job created are much lower than in any other sector. For example, in 1992 the cost of creating a job in the metallurgical industry was the equivalent of $419 400; in the agricultural sector $12 980; in livestock $11 180; and in afforestation activities $7260 (Abrahao and Furtado, 1992).

3.10 Legal aspects of afforestation

Although many laws have been introduced in Brazil to protect the native forests, few have been put into practice. Other more pressing priorities receive far greater attention, ranging from unemployment and running water to social conflicts and poverty. Environmental matters are now being taken more seriously, however, than in the past.

Various laws have recently been introduced which are specifically aimed at stimulating afforestation and protecting both the native forests and the environment at the same time. The Federal Law No.97 628 of 12 April 1989 requires that by the year 1995 all charcoal must be produced from plantations. This law, however, allows the production of up to 20 per cent of charcoal from residues and hence in any given case the amount of charcoal to be produced from plantations should not exceed 80 per cent. Unfortunately this law is unrealistic, since the target would have required planting 300 000ha annually from the late 1980s if charcoal demand was to be met from plantations alone. The amount required is far higher than the present annual estimated planting area of between 100 000 and 150 000ha/yr. With no clear policy of afforestation, and without fiscal incentives, afforestation on a large scale in the immediate future does not look probable even in the state of MG unless a new policy is put in place.

New legislative changes have been introduced in the Federal Code giving each state more autonomy and control over its own forestry policy. The Forestry Law of MG (Law 10 561 of December 1991), for example, pays considerably more attention to environmental aspects. This new law makes it possible to have a greater control over who can exploit native forests and how in the future. Whether this law can be enforced remains to be seen. It is important to create a balance, however, to prevent too many regulations that could also have a negative effect on the whole industry. There is already growing concern with this kind of legislation that is forcing a rethink about the long-term future of the charcoal industry, particularly among small charcoal producers.

An important aim of the new law is to ensure the sustainable exploitation of the remaining native forests and to maintain biodiversity. Anyone who wants to explore or cut a particular forest must, in theory at least, submit a very detailed plan to the state's Forestry Institute for approval. The proposal must state clearly what is intended and for what purpose with information on volume of wood to be cut, species used, and for what end. The Institute authorities have the final say on whether or not a particular project goes ahead. If cutting and pruning is allowed, no further exploration would be permitted until the original forest reaches at least 80 per cent of its original volume which would take at least 12 years (Lei Florestal, 1991; Macedo, personal communication, 1994).

4. Technical Aspects of Charcoal Production

4.1 Fundamentals

There are many definitions of charcoal, but few of them are very precise or authoritative. Emrich (1985) defines charcoal as 'the residue of solid non-agglomerating organic matter, of vegetable or animal origin, that results from carbonization by heat in the absence of air at a temperature above 300°C. This definition distinguishes charcoal from coke, which is formed by the carbonization of fluid organic matter such as plastic coal or petroleum (when heated, coking coal becomes plastic before carbonization). It also distinguishes between bituminous coals and lignite, because they have not been subject to carbonizing temperatures during their transformation.

Charcoal is made by carbonizing wood (wood pyrolysis), during which most of the volatile components of wood are eliminated; this process is also called 'dry wood distillation'. During the process there is an increase in carbon content in the charcoal from about 50 per cent to about 75 per cent, partly a result of the reduction of hydrogen and oxygen in the wood; this process is also called 'wood carbonization'.

During the conversion from wood to charcoal important physio-chemical changes take place, a result of the different temperatures at which the process takes place. For example, between 100 and 170°C most of the water is evaporated; between 170 and 270°C gases are emitted containing CO and CO_2, condensable vapours which form pyrolysis oil after scrubbing and chilling; between 270 and 280°C an exothermic reaction starts, which can be detected by the spontaneous generation of heat and the rising temperature (Emrich, 1985).

Different temperatures result in different yields of charcoal. At temperatures of 300°C charcoal yield is about 50 per cent. At carbonization temperatures of 500 to 600°C the volatiles are lower and retort yields are around 30 per cent. At very high temperatures (about 1000°C) the volatile content is almost zero and yields fall to about 25 per cent (Trossero, 1991).

Thus the application of heat and its control to produce charcoal is a key factor, one which determines which process should be used. Many heating systems have been tried in the past, but three basic types have survived the long history of charcoal-making:

(a) internal heating by controlled combustion of the raw material;

(b) external heating by combustion of firewood, fuel oil, or natural gas; and

22

(c) heating with circulated gas (retort or converter gas).

Internal-heating systems are the most commonly used in Brazil. Part of the raw material is burnt under controlled air inlet conditions. For charcoal production a temperature of 400°C is recommended, from which about 40 per cent of the initial weight of the wood is converted to charcoal, with 77 per cent of fixed carbon (Moreira et al., 1992). The heat of combustion provides the necessary temperature. About 10 to 20 per cent of the wood (by weight) is sacrificed to generate the energy to maintain the process. This is the main system used in Brazil, where about 60 per cent of the wood (by weight) is converted into gases and then released into the atmosphere (Brito, 1990).

External-heating systems and heating with circulated gas are still little known in Brazil, but some experiments have been carried out with the traditional Beehive Brick Kiln which have shown potential productivity increases of as much as 30 per cent. Much greater efforts have been put into developing the retort system, because it can produce charcoal on a large industrial scale, of higher quality, and with better use of by-products (see Chapter 8.3).

4.2 Charcoal-making technology

As stated earlier, there are many techniques, both simple and sophisticated, for producing charcoal. In its simplest form wood is burnt in an open fire and the charred remains are recovered as charcoal. A more controlled method of manufacturing charcoal is by restricting the supply of air during carbonization. Two main methods are traditionally used:

(a) stacking the timber on the ground and covering it with soil, often referred as an earth-clamp or earth-mound kiln; and

(b) digging a hole into which the timber is placed and which is then covered with soil, commonly referred to as a pit kiln (Hollingdale et al., 1991).

Efficiencies and quality are usually very low, although they may alter in response to local conditions, timber species, climatic conditions, tools and manpower, and charcoal-making knowledge. Although it is difficult to provide authoritative figures, as charcoal production efficiency estimates vary considerably, in general, a major characteristic of Brazilian charcoal production is poor efficiency (on a weight-by-weight basis) and low productivity. (This is also the case in many other parts of the world. For example, about 12 per cent is normal in Zambia, 11 to 15 per cent in Tanzania, and 9 to 12 per cent in Kenya.) But in the most efficient kilns (those used in plantations), efficiency is about 30 per cent and in some cases 35 per cent, quite high compared with many other parts of the world. Efficiency of charcoal production varies so much because it depends not only on the type of kiln being used, but also on the type of wood being carbonized, its moisture content, the density and diameter of the wood, and other factors.

Generally, all species of wood can be carbonized to produce charcoal, although the quality can vary. The moisture content of some wood has to be lowered by burning extra wood. This lowers the overall charcoal yield, so the higher the water content, the lower the yield. Freshly produced charcoal contains almost no moisture, but if it is left exposed to the air or water it can absorb considerable moisture.

Because of the low conversion efficiency of wood to charcoal, together with the high cost of transport, charcoal is produced near forests. In the case of native forests this is a very dispersed activity and charcoal is produced in small amounts, usually no more than 500 tonnes per year at any given site. Charcoal from forest plantations, however, can be produced on a much larger scale – about 10 000 to 20 000 tonnes per year per *carvoaria*. With this large-scale production of charcoal, it makes more sense economically to use more advanced equipment, such as retorts, to take advantage of the by-products. Investment costs are high, and without a market for such products, this option may not be attractive to the large charcoal producer.

Charcoal-making is in many ways a wasteful process, since during the carbonization process only 30 to 40 per cent of the wood is actually converted to charcoal, and the rest is released into the atmosphere in the form of gases. It is estimated that with modern carbonization techniques, for each tonne of charcoal produced, about 0.6 tonnes of dehydrated chemical products and $7 \times 10^6 J$ of energy in the form of poor quality gas – currently partially burned inside the kilns or released into the atmosphere – could be recovered (Rivelli and Rezende, 1989; Rezende et al., 1993). Moreira et al., (1992) quoting figures from the Santa Barbara company, state that only about 42 per cent of the energy represented by the crop in the field is retained in the final product.

If one excludes plantations, charcoal is still being produced in many cases with primitive technology, little operational control of kilns, manual loading and unloading, and without quantitative and qualitative control. It operates in an empirical and craftsman-like way with a labour force that is poorly educated, if not illiterate, which makes it more difficult to modernize the sector (Brito, 1990; Brito, 1991; Rivelli and Rezende, 1989). This is particularly the case with regard to small charcoal production from native forests.

4.3 Masonry kilns in commercial charcoal production

Brazilian charcoal is produced in one of several different types of masonry kilns, ranging from the simple kilns used by small charcoal-producers, to the big mechanized or semi-mechanized kilns used by the large companies.

The advantages of the masonry kilns are that they are relatively inexpensive and, because of their operational simplicity, a local work-force can be used. The use of more complex industrial systems to manufacture charcoal in large quantities may result in the recovery of chemicals or other by-products, but they will also result in higher investment costs, including higher capital and skilled labour costs, and at the moment have not attracted the same attention as the masonry kiln.

Of the various types of kilns in operation in Brazil, two are the most common: the *rabo-quente* (hot tail) kiln, and the *superficie* or *colmeia* (surface or beehive) brick kiln. One other type, the *encosta* or *barranco* (slope-type) kiln, is in fact a variation of the beehive brick kiln. The first two types are described briefly below, and Table 4.1 gives details of a typical industrial kiln in Brazil, together with charcoal conversion efficiencies.

The *rabo-quente* kiln is built with common bricks, usually without a chimney, and with one door. It has an effective kiln volume holding between 4.5t (the most commonly used) and 250t of wood. The kiln diameter varies from 3 to 7m, and it is 3.5 to 3.7m high; the chopped wood length varies between 1.2 and 1.5m. Kilns are grouped in *baterias* (batteries), which are normally made up of six to eight kilns. The *bateria* is controlled by two people or one family. Sometimes it is a migrant activity, subcontracted out by farmers who want to clean the land for pasture or agriculture. This type of kiln is the most widely used to produce charcoal from native forests.

The *superficie* or *colmeia* kiln is also built with common bricks, but it has between one and six chimneys and one or two doors. The effective kiln volume holds between 17.5t (the most common type) and 75t of wood; the base diameter varies between 5 and 8m and the height between 3.2 and 5m (Brito, 1990). The main advantage of the large kiln is the fact that it allows a certain degree of mechanization, enabling trucks to load and unload inside the kiln, for example.

Most of the charcoal produced from eucalyptus plantations is made in surface beehive-type kilns, which are often grouped in *carvoarias*, comprising 20 to 40 kilns, sometimes more. These sites have water, sewage, and one or two houses for the supervisors. Some of these *carvoarias* are organized into batteries of eight kilns, to divide the work (two people per battery of 40m^3 kilns), or to organize tar extraction when practised. The useful life of a typical kiln is four to 10 years.

The costs of these commercial beehive kilns in MG vary between $900 and $1200. If the cost for building infrastructure (which is almost always the case) is included, then costs per kiln would be about $2000 to $2400.

Most kilns are internally heated, although the modern types can be heated externally. They are built of ordinary bricks and mortar made from clay, and are often made locally at the *carvoarias* by the operators themselves, thus keeping the costs low.

To illustrate the commercial techniques of manufacturing charcoal from eucalyptus plantations, examples from three leading charcoal producing companies, Acesita, Mannesmann, and Belgo-Mineira, are described.

Acesita uses a design with an external combustion chamber connected to the kiln floor by channels. The chamber was intended to maximize forest use by burning residues, but because of the high harvesting costs of residues the chamber is only used to ignite and control the process. The kiln has six side chimneys and no side holes. The wall is vertical, with a domed ceiling. Most kilns are 2m high and 5m in diameter. New kilns are being built with 2.2m-high walls to allow a small tractor to enter and load the charcoal.

The cycle begins by filling the kilns through the door, standing the logs on their ends (the logs are as long as the height of the wall). Some wood is added to fill the round top, but not much as the operators want to save as much time as possible so that the wood loading can be completed in one day. The door is closed and a small amount of wood is burned in the combustion chamber to ignite the kiln. Once the ignition operation is complete, the whole carbonization process is controlled by the amount of air that is allowed to enter through the combustion chamber. After carbonization is complete, the chamber and the top of the chimneys are closed and the kiln is left to cool by itself. No water injection is needed. The overall process takes place as follows: one day for unloading and loading, three days for carbonization, and three days for cooling.

A kiln with an external chamber permits better control of the process and greatly reduces labour costs. One man can control the whole carbonization process in a *carvoaria* of 40 kilns, because he does not have to close several side holes with mortar, but only one chamber door per kiln.

Acesita Energetica has also developed a compact masonry kiln which incorporates tar recovery. The tar recuperation system is attached to eight kilns – four of which are used at any given time to carbonize wood, while the other four are used to cool the charcoal. The fumes from each of the four kilns are collected and then piped out to a sealed box. The fumes are washed with the recycling liquids then collected. This system can recover about 120kg of tar per tonne of charcoal.

Mannesmann Forestal has also begun a programme aimed specifically at improving charcoal production and efficiency at all levels. A new rectangular kiln (of the type used in Missouri, USA) with capacities of about 22 to 36 tonnes of wood is being developed, with good results so far. In this model it is possible to produce 63 tonnes of charcoal per month, compared with 15 tonnes with the smaller circular model; both models have a similar efficiency of about 30 to 35 per cent (weight-by-weight oven dry basis). With good carbonization, almost 84kg of tar per tonne of charcoal can be recovered (Nogueira and Oliveira, 1991). Mechanizing charcoal production is an important goal, to relieve the labour force of the most difficult and exhausting manual tasks.

The rectangular kiln allows a certain degree of mechanization, such as trucks entering to load and unload (although at the moment unloading is done manually), and it also allows greater temperature control, which could enable an increase in the conversion efficiency of wood from the present 30 per cent to about 35 per cent in the near future. Efficiencies, wood moisture content, wood density, reduced charcoal fines, and the total production cycle, are all being investigated and monitored (Nogueira et al, 1991; Nogueira and Oliveira, 1991).

Mannesmann is planning to build kilns with external chambers, using a similar design as Acesita. The cost for such a unit is $2400, including all infrastructure costs. Charcoal production from this type of *carvoaria* is around 750 to 875 tonnes per month, using 11 workers. The useful life of these kilns is close to five years.

Mannesmann still uses the *rabo quente* kilns, with side holes but without chimneys. Investment costs are about 20 per cent lower than Acesita's external chamber model, with equivalent production. It does requires over 50 per cent more labour, however, because the side-hole kilns require more labour to control operations during night and weekend work. The full cycle of such kilns is normally nine days – one for loading/unloading, four for burning, and four for cooling. The useful life is about four years, but this can be extended with some minor modifications (Furtado, personal communication and 1992).

Belgo-Mineira, Brazil's largest producer of pig-iron through its subsidiary CAF (which is responsible for plantation forestry and charcoal production), has opted for building *carvoarias* with better infrastructure and permanence as a production centre. The kiln wall and domed ceiling is reinforced with steel and cement. The kilns are quite large, eight metres in diameter, permitting inside mechanical unloading and loading operations. The cooling period is decreased by spraying water inside the kiln. Such kilns have a working life of 10 years. Since Belgo-Mineira's recent decision to shift gradually to coke, however, its charcoal R&D programme is now in doubt.

4.4 Material balance and charcoal yield

Wood density, moisture content, and calorific value are all important factors that affect charcoal production and quality, but have received relatively little attention in the past. Research is now also being carried out to discover the most suitable eucalyptus species for charcoal production. *E. grandis*, for example, which formed the bulk of the early plantations (because it grows fast and is well suited to many parts of Brazil), is not considered the most suitable wood for charcoal production because of its low density. *E. camaldulensis*, despite its lower growth rate, has a much higher wood density, and therefore is preferred for charcoal production. *E. camaldulensis* has 82 per cent higher productivity per tonne of pig-iron/ha of plantation than *E. grandis* (Mannesmann Forestal; Nogueira and Oliveira, 1991).

A number of excellent studies have been published in recent years on many aspects of eucalypts in Brazil, illustrating the considerable knowledge that Brazilians have acquired in forest management (Barros and Novais, 1990; Lima, 1993).

The moisture content of wood is also being monitored more closely, and research is being conducted to determine the optimal moisture of air-dried wood. Juvillar and Nogueira (1988) found that the quantity and quality of charcoal is proportional to both the moisture content and quality of the wood. The overall extra cost of drying the wood is more than compensated for by the additional gains in charcoal production.

Determining the efficiency, productivity, yield, etc., of wood is not an easy matter since they depend on many factors. Both wood and charcoal are measured in various different units, such as solid steres, cubic metres, tonnes, stacked steres, etc., (see Appendix 2). Thus, in order to calculate gravimetric yields one has to take into account losses from the conversion from steres of wood to weight; then when the wood is converted to charcoal, density and quality will also influence the final yield.

Charcoal quality can be expressed in terms of 'fixed carbon content', which can range from about 50 to 95 per cent and will have a strong influence on the final yield. Quality is very important, but producing better charcoal (i.e. with a higher fixed carbon content) results in an overall loss in productivity.

The fixed carbon content is the most important constituent in metallurgy, since it is the fixed carbon which is responsible for reducing the iron oxides in the iron-ore to produce metal. A balance must be achieved, however, between the fireable nature of high fixed-carbon charcoal, and the greater strength of charcoal with lower fixed-carbon and higher variable matter content, to obtain optimum blast furnace operation (Trossero, 1991; Grandin et al., 1991) (see also section 4.5).

The energy efficiency of the carbonization process improves greatly if the fixed carbon content of the charcoal is reduced. Mannesmann estimates that as much as 51 per cent of energy losses occur if fixed carbon is kept at 85 per cent. The gains in energy are contained in the volatiles, which are then transported to the steel mill. In an integrated plant, where blast furnace gas is used in the process, this improvement in fixed carbon represents a gain in energy. For the independent pig-iron producer who uses roughly half of the gas in the heating stage and loses the rest in the process, such losses are of little concern. Thus the best type of charcoal to produce depends very much on the end use to which it will be put.

28

Research on all aspects of charcoal production and use in Brazil is only about a decade old. Nonetheless there are already a number of public and private institutions which are investigating many different aspects of charcoal production and use, such as wood and charcoal quality, improved carbonization systems, metallic and rectangular kilns, retorts for the continuous carbonization of wood, and the better use of by-products.

It is clear, however, that the modernization and improvement of charcoal production and use must be a major research priority in the future. The tasks that require urgent attention are increased biomass production by the plantations of appropriate species to produce good quality charcoal; the mechanization of the industry to relieve the labour force of the more difficult physical tasks and increase their living standards; and improved reduction efficiency of charcoal. The better use of by-products will also have to play a major role in providing additional income, easing the modernization process, and reducing environmental impacts.

4.5 Charcoal versus coke

Currently about two-thirds of Brazil's pig-iron is produced in large-scale coke blast furnaces and about one-third in smaller scale charcoal blast furnaces of about $560m^3$ (140 tonnes) capacity. The processes for making pig-iron using either coke or charcoal blast furnaces are basically similar, with only a few significant differences (see Table 4.2). Both charcoal and coke are used as reductor and thermal agents. The main differences between charcoal and coke lies in their physical, chemical, and metallurgical properties (Gradin et al., 1991).

Both physical and chemical properties are of considerable importance for industrial charcoal, as they constitute major cost components. The physical properties of charcoal influence the output of the blast furnace, whereas the chemical properties are more related to the amount of charcoal needed per tonne of iron and the composition of the finished product. Blast furnace charcoal must be strong in compression to withstand the crashing load of the blast furnace charge of 'burden'. This compression strength (much lower than that of coke) determines the practical height, and hence the efficiency and output of the blast furnace (Trossero, 1991).

The main charcoal properties which affect the operation of a blast furnace are: chemical composition; density (which is intrinsically linked to that of the the wood – the higher the density the lower the charcoal consumption); and charcoal – the size of which can vary from 5mm to over 100mm, but should be on average about 40mm (Assis et al., 1982).

Table 4.3 shows variations in charcoal composition as found in the blast furnace charge in a large charcoal-based plant of Belgo Mineira, MG. The charcoal was produced in a beehive brick kiln from a mixture of 60 per cent wood from homogeneous native forests and 40 per cent from eucalyptus plantations.

Coke typically contains more mineral impurities than charcoal, and therefore produces lower quality iron. Coke-fired smelting also requires higher temperatures, on average about 1500°C compared to 1400°C for charcoal, so it is used mostly in large furnaces.

Apart from physical and chemical characteristics, there are other important factors in setting up a new plant. These include investment costs, scale of production, social considerations, and environmental factors. For example, coke use requires more capital to build the coke ovens, while charcoal uses less capital but requires more labour. In 1991 the costs of coke (at factory gate) were about \$247/t, while those of charcoal varied between \$30 and \$31/m^3. At this coke price charcoal would be competitive at about \$50/m^3 (Ferreira, personal communication). Charcoal appears to be much more environmentally acceptable than coke, as it is thought that the fumes from coke are an important contributor to acid rain because of the high sulphur content, which does not apply to charcoal since wood contains very little sulphur.

The transportation of charcoal, usually for very long distances in Brazil, usually reduces about 30 to 35 per cent (or even more) of the total volume to fines of less than 9.5mm, which cannot be fed into the top of the blast furnace (Grandin et al., 1991). But the use of charcoal fines also allows the complementary use of coke with higher ash content. Although the use of charcoal fines is not new (their use dates back to the 1880s), studies in Brazil since the 1980s have shown that charcoal fines can have both important economic and environmental advantages.

Many of the coke-based power plants around the world need to be modernized to meet new environmental requirements. This is a costly exercise (with estimates of about \$500M needed to build a new plant with a capacity of about 0.8M tonnes/year). Recent Brazilian legislation means that emissions from new coke plants must not exceed 80mg/Nm^3 of SOx and 5mg/Nm^3 for NOx. Plants currently in operation in Brazil emit about 150mg/Nm^3 for SOx and NOx (Heinisch, 1991).

Thus not only economic, but also environmental factors will be at the centre of any discussion. In Brazil, charcoal seems to be the natural choice for the steel-making industry because the country lacks good quality coal, and coke has to be imported. Charcoal is also a good reductor and thermal agent and has many socio-economic ramifications, and it is environmentally more acceptable than coke if produced renewably (see also 7.1). The industry, however, needs to modernize all its phases, from planting, to charcoal-making, to end use, if it is to have a long-term future.

5. Charcoal Production Costs

Charcoal production costs do not appear to have been an overriding concern in the past. Only during the past decade have costs been taken more seriously, and some detailed studies have been carried out by Cardoso Vale and Nascimento (1989), Rezende and Cardoso (1989), and Valente et al., (1991).

Brazilian charcoal production falls into two main groups. In the first group are the small charcoal producers, usually poor rural people or small farmers. Charcoal is an additional, and often subsistence activity. Their source of wood is the native forests, but very frequently residues from the expansion of agriculture and pastures are also used. Efficiency and economic costs are not very relevant.

In the second group we find the more professional charcoal producers. Their main source of wood is the industrial plantations, and they tend to be employees of either a large charcoal producer and commercial enterprise or, more often, a subcontractor of such a company. Efficiency and economic costs are central to their operations.

Forestry and charcoal costs can vary considerably as they are site-specific and are influenced by many factors, including local climate, topography, and transport. Brazilian charcoal is not as cheap in Brazil as one might expect, considering the large scale of charcoal production and industrial applications. This is partly explained by the high transport costs and the low efficiency at almost all levels, particularly where native forests are the raw material. The cost of charcoal is the single most important item in the cost of pig-iron production, usually accounting for over 50 per cent of the bill. The Santa Barbara company, for example, quote the following pig-iron production figures: charcoal: 65 per cent; capital: 14 per cent; raw material: 10 per cent; and labour and services 11 per cent (Moreira et al., 1992).

In this section we examine charcoal production under different conditions: the cost of forest plantations and native forests in MG; forest plantation costs in the Carajas region; the use of charcoal from native forests in the Amazon (unsustainable production); and charcoal from Sustainable Forest Management Projects, also in the Carajas region. This will give an overall view of different charcoal production costs in the most important charcoal producing areas of the country.

Harvesting, carbonization, and transport are the most significant items in the final cost of charcoal, but forest productivity is also an important factor

31

(Rezende et al., 1987). Prices can fluctuate widely, however, and often reflect market conditions rather than real production costs. Average prices of charcoal from native forests in December 1991, for example, were as low as $10.70/m^3 in Bahia, and as high as $16.80/m^3 in Santos Dumont (MG), down from $27.80/m^3 in April of the same year (ABRACAVE, 1992). In 1992 charcoal prices remained steady in dollar terms – between $12 and $21/m^3, or $48 to $84/tonne (ABRACAVE, 1993). The dollar prices do not reflect the real costs, however, given the frequent and large devaluations of the Cruzeiro against the dollar and the high inflation rates. Table 5.1 summarizes charcoal prices for 1992 and the previous decade.

Cardoso Vale and Nascimento (1989) calculated that the cost of charcoal in areas of good topography was about $19/m^3, and in difficult terrain was about $23/m^3 in 1989 dollars. They also calculated that the establishment cost of eucalyptus plantations (for a lifespan of one to 22 years), was $1308 per hectare.

Campos and Toninello (1989) concluded that at a market price of $30/m^3 of charcoal, forests with productivity levels below 18m^3 (4.5 tonnes of wood/ha/yr) and at distances of over 300km from the consumption centres, would not be economic under Brazilian conditions. One of the authors, Furtado, carried out a field survey in 1991 on the cost of charcoal production with Mannesmann Forestal (see Table 5.2). The costs were about $28/m^3 ($112/tonne) of charcoal, made up of wood: $9, harvesting: $9.50, carbonization: $5.80, and transport (304km) $3.80. These figures can be regarded as minimum costs for well-managed forestry companies with good productivity. Similar costs can be obtained from other well-managed companies, such as Acesita and Belgo-Mineira. We conclude that overall the cost of charcoal from plantations is $27 to $31 per m^3 ($108 to $124 per tonne) of charcoal. In areas with lower productivities and less well-managed forests, the costs will be much higher and vary widely.

Table 5.3 shows the estimated costs of charcoal from the eastern Amazon region, which is produced on an unsustainable basis. The site, near Paragominas (PA), consists of a farm (Fazenda Agua Parada) of 25 000ha which used mostly tree-clearing residues from the expansion of agricultural and pasture land. The low cost is partly a result of the fact that charcoal producers do not pay, or pay very low prices, for their raw material. The kilns they use are of the traditional beehive brick type. The kiln-sites have a lifespan of about one year and produce about 3000m^3 (650 tonnes) of charcoal. Charcoal production is approximately 1500m^3/ha/yr (375 tonnes) and in 1984 there were about 500 kilns employing 250 people. The main advantages of this area to the charcoal producer include a reasonably good transport infrastructure, good topography, a plentiful supply of labour, and a low incidence of malaria. Some disadvantages include transport difficulties during the rainy season, the lack of running

Modern forest plantations enable charcoal producers to plant the best species for the job.

water, land ownership problems, the high cost of basic amenities, and the lack of charcoal-making experience.

Another site near Maraba (PA) has good topography, large landholdings, and timber extraction rights. It has great forestry potential and wood is for the most part free. The problems are similar to the Paragominas site, with high operational costs because of high tree density, but with some additional labour supply problems and a high incidence of malaria. The two main advantages are the abundance of raw material and the lower transport costs resulting from the shorter distances to the consuming centre.

The charcoal from the Paragominas region was sold to a cement factory 280km away, and that from Maraba for pig-iron smelting. Although this study dates back to 1984, it is still representative of that region, since charcoal production methods remain largely unchanged. Charcoal production does not, according to the information reported, seem to be a very profitable enterprise, considering the low return on investment.

Table 5.4 summarizes the estimated charcoal production costs from a sustainable forest management project, 'Fazenda Descoberta', which operates a 15-year rotation period. The cost of charcoal production has been reduced quite considerably through a number of measures, including improved productivity, better management, and administrative changes. Total direct costs have been cut from $77/tonne in 1991 to $53 to $58/tonne in November 1993. These costs exclude financial and structural costs. Financial costs are estimated to be about $6 per tonne. Total direct costs are expected to fall to about \$52 to \$56 per tonne in the short term, and financial costs to about \$2.80 to \$3.20/tonne (Belo Elian, personal communication; Cardoso Vale, personal communication).

Charcoal is a major component of the final product cost in the industries that use it, and costs are comparatively high in Brazil. The charcoal-making industry pays very low wages (although higher than similar unskilled jobs) and a large proportion of charcoal is still produced from native forests and from forestry and agricultural clearings, which continue to have a low value. Thus the only way to lower costs is to make greater investments and produce a better-trained labour force. This means higher investment costs in both skilled and semi-skilled workers (who would have to be better paid) and on new technology, which will have to be offset by increases in productivity.

It is still cheaper to produce charcoal from native forests than from plantations, despite the high transport costs, so the large industrial charcoal consumers often prefer to purchase charcoal from small independent producers rather than from their own modern plantations. Charcoal is produced on plantations because of legal requirements, but charcoal from the small independent producers will continue to be both an economically and financially attractive option to the large charcoal consumers – partly because they do not have to pay for all the associated costs of establishing and maintaining the plantation forests.

As the native forests are progressively depleted costs will increase, particularly in MG, if the planned afforestation projects fail to materialize. If the demand for charcoal was to increase significantly in the near future, it could create a serious supply problem for the iron and steel industry. For MG in particular, two main options are possible: increase productivity at all levels (from forest to end product) so that major gains can be made by decreasing demand for charcoal while at the same time increasing wood supply, but without increasing the planted area or the use of native forests; or maintain (or reduce) iron and steel capacity while increasing productivity and efficiency so that demand for charcoal remains steady or decreases.

In the Carajas region of the Amazon the situation is quite different, as there is an abundant supply of wood and the demand for charcoal is smaller. Because charcoal production is a new activity in the region, and with tougher law enforcement, more rational use of the forests should be possible. The sustainable production of charcoal from native forests in the short term, and a combination of plantations and native forest in the longer term, should keep the supply of wood and charcoal at reasonable levels (see Chapter 6).

6. The Future Challenge: The Need For Sustainable And Rational Use Of Native Forests

6.1 Carajas

The Carajas region comprises 25Mha of the Amazon, from the states of Maranhao, Para, and Tocantins, along the San Luis-Carajas Railway. The combination of the lack of coal in this very iron-ore rich region, the high transport costs associated with coal, and the region's great potential for charcoal production, were all determining factors in promoting charcoal-based iron plants. The main difference between this region and the rest of Brazil is that, by law at least, charcoal production is required to be based on sound silvicultural methods, through either the sustained management of natural forests and/or afforestation. The goal is to reforest one million hectares with different agro-silvicultural projects and to preserve and recover at least another 0.3Mha (ASICA, 1991).

The socio-economic horizon of the Carajas region changed dramatically with the discovery of large mineral resources in the Sierra dos Carajas. This has opened up new opportunities and presented new challenges not only in terms of its enormous mineral preserves (it has 40 per cent of Brazil's iron ore reserves – some 18 billion tonnes, and 75 per cent of its copper – 1.2 billion tonnes) (Grupo Itaminas, 1991), but also in terms of the enormous investments already made in infrastructure, and equipment.

Colonization in the area of the Projeto Grande Carajas (excluding the Sao Luis–Santa Ines area which was already colonized), was greatly stimulated by the opening of the road Brasilia–Para (BR–010), which made large areas of Southern Para and Western Maranhao accessible. The occupation was chaotic and unplanned and the main economic activities were based on wood extraction and cattle ranching. This led to serious social conflicts, rapid population increases, the deforestation of large areas, and soil degradation. The construction of new roads, such as the Transamazonica, further accelerated this process. By 1986, just before the first pig-iron smelter was built, about 9.5Mha was estimated to have been deforested already, which represented 38 per cent of the land area under the influence of the Projeto Grande Carajas. More recent estimates put the total deforested area at about 8.5Mha (ASICA, 1991).

The social structure remains fragile and explosive because the different colonization projects have attracted tens of thousands of migrants. Many of the early projects failed, forcing thousands of people to find subsistence employment, such as working as *garimpo* in the mines or exploiting the forests, or migrating to the cities. During the period of 1980 to 1987 the urban population in the region increased by 21 per cent and it is now one of the poorest in Brazil, with a high degree of both malnutrition and illiteracy. The estimated population along the corridor is about 1.25M (Grupo Itaminas, 1991).

In the initial projections of Grande Carajas, it was planned to have an installed capacity of 1.5M tonnes/year of pig-iron during the first phase, and a charcoal consumption of 1.5M tonnes/year. These projections were never achieved, and the 1993 installed capacity was 614 000 tonnes/year with charcoal consumption of 430 000 tonnes/year, spread between five companies. New plants are expected to begin operating in the future, which may increase this capacity to about 1M tonnes of pig-iron annually. Although these quantities are smaller than the second rank states which produce pig-iron, the fact that they are located in the Amazon focused world attention on the possible destruction of native forests.

The introduction of pig-iron works to the area in the mid-1980s brought a new situation to the Carajas region. Although the charcoal-based steel sector initially used mainly residues from sawmills and forest clearings from agriculture and pasture expansion, this was regarded as a short-term solution to the supply of wood for raw material. Afforestation then began in the early 1980s by Companhia Vale Rio Doce (CVRD), with studies being carried out on more than 150 different species. The best results were obtained with eucalypts, of which 39 species were investigated. Four species have proved to be the most suitable for the region: *E.urophylla, E.pellita, E.tereticornis,* and *E. camaldulensis.* Some experimental results indicated productivities of about 6.75t/ha/yr, about $27m^3$. Establishment costs are quite high though – about $1560/ha for the first seven years, ($912 for the production of seedlings and soil preparation, and $478 for planting and maintenance) (ASICA, 1991).

There appear to be three main options open to the charcoal-based steel industry in the Carajas region:

(a) Use of forest residues. Currently this represents about 96 per cent of charcoal production (52 per cent from sawmills, 44 per cent from farming and cattle expansion, and 4 per cent directly from native forests) (ASICA, 1991). There is a considerable amount of residue being generated by the sawmills at the moment that has little economic value apart from charcoal. Although it is an attractive alternative, it can only be regarded as a short-term and transitory solution, since large areas have already been deforested, so clearing supplies are bound to decrease. In addition, the introduction of new and more efficient technologies in sawmills will reduce the availability of such residues. Another possibility which has also been considered is the use of babassu nut residues, but this option does not seem to be very promising, at least in the short term, because of the dispersed nature of this resource. There is a growing recognition among experts, however, that this could be a real alternative in the medium to long term.

(b) Afforestation of already degraded lands. Large-scale afforestation for charcoal production appears to be a viable alternative, but this would be a medium- to long-term option. It is also quite expensive to reforest because of poor quality soils, pest and disease problems, and lack of experience.

(c) Sustainable forest management projects. This appears the most promising alternative, given the forest potential of the region. It may be of vital importance for the survival of the forests, since it will result in an increased economic value which the forests lack today. Without any economic value it is thought that the forest will, quite simply, disappear as a result of other socio-economic pressures. Most companies established in the region recognize this potential and are involved in some kind of 'Sustainable Forest Management Pilot Project' (SFMPP).

A major difficulty with this approach is the lack of experience and detailed knowledge of this type of exploitation, which makes it currently uncertain. The idea is to cut between 40 and 50 per cent of the standing stock on a rotational basis, then to allow the native forests to fully recover, which is expected to take 10 to 15 years, before the next extraction cycle begins again.

In summary, the Carajas region has an enormous potential to develop integrated industrial projects, particularly iron and steel. The production of

Small producers will often pay little, or nothing, for their supplies.

charcoal-based pig-iron could form the basis for industrial production of semi-finished and finished products on a large industrial scale.

6.2 The sustainable forest management concept

Sustainable forest management is not yet a proven system and it has its critics, mainly because of disagreement about the capacity of the native forest to regenerate (at least in economic terms), the time scale required, and so forth. Forestry projects are of a long-term nature, requiring large capital investment (depending on the nature of the project) and large areas of land. This means that in most cases such projects can only be undertaken by large corporations. Large-scale afforestation projects have been seriously criticized in the past, and experiments with smaller units are now being undertaken, such as the Fazendeiro Forestal project in MG.

The present irrational destruction of the forests and the resulting implications have, for years now, been amply publicized and thus we do not need to enter into details here. There is no justification, either on economic or ecological grounds, to substitute existing tropical forests with eucalyptus or any other species, because of the climatic conditions of the region (high temperature and humidity, and the risk of pests and diseases to name some). There is also little experience with large-scale plantations in the region, except for Jari, which was originally a disaster (Fearnside and Rankin, 1980; Fearnside and Rankin, 1985; Fearnside, 1988), and it will therefore require much longer to investigate and understand all the problems associated with modern silviculture. Many lessons have been learned from the Jari venture.

There is enormous forestry potential in the region, which is far from being fully realized. Indigenous forests are still regarded as an obstacle to development, for example, and agricultural and cleared land today has a value of about three times that of forest land. This negative attitude will undoubtedly change if society realizes the full economic potential of the forests, and stops burning them. For example, in 1988 it was estimated that the wood contained in the forests burned in Brazil was worth over $9 billion in the domestic market and over $55 billion if such wood was exported (Folha de Sao Paulo, 1989). It is therefore very important to find an economic value for existing forests, as this will be the best guarantee for their survival. Charcoal production, although it may not be the most noble end of the wood in forests, can play a major role along with other products in using and maintaining large areas of native tropical forests.

Thus, the sustainable production of charcoal from these forests may be a partial answer to their irrational destruction. By this we mean 'the rational utilization of native forests with the maximum possible economic return and with the lowest possible environmental risk'. Of course, this is easier said than done! The exploitation of native forests must be done in such a way as to create the conditions that would allow native forests to regrow relatively quickly. Sustainable development must take into account many different factors, including economic and environmental pressures, soil nutrients, ecological equilibrium, fauna, and soil erosion.

The capacity of the Amazon forests for regrowth will be of vital importance to the economic viability of sustainable development projects. Generally, when a forest is cut the regeneration/re-colonization begins with the so-called pioneer trees (fast growing trees), eventually culminating in the regrowth of the old forest after varying lengths of time. The pioneer trees require much light for growth and can rapidly modify soil conditions, allowing other less light-demanding species to emerge in the shade and thus eventually re-establishing the forest in its original form.

The speed with which this process can take place depends on a number of factors – man's intervention, plot size, density of and cutting rates, among other things. This will happen relatively quickly if the areas of forest cut are not large, and if human intervention is not excessive in the natural regeneration process. Much research is still needed to determine the optimum regeneration conditions under different situations.

It must be remarked, however, that sustainable forest development does not necessarily mean allowing the old forests to re-establish themselves in their former condition; it may involve selection of certain varieties, perhaps with less total biodiversity, in order to meet specific requirements.

6.3 The Sustainable Forest Management Project of 'Fazenda: Descoberta'

This farm is located about 120km north-east of Acelandia, in the State of Maranhao, near the Para State. It has 16 665ha, is owned by the Cia Siderurgica Vale do Pindare, and constitutes a good example of an attempt at charcoal production from humid tropical forests on a sustainable and rational basis. This *fazenda* was bought by the company in the mid-1980s and has shown a very strong commitment to sustainable charcoal production from native forests. It is an interesting and promising experiment which, if successful, could have important consequences for the region in general and the pig-iron industry in particular.

The main objective of the experiment at the Fazenda Descoberta is the sustainable production of charcoal to supply the company's pig-iron plant in Acelandia. Regeneration is expected to be rapid because the reduction, or even depletion, of certain species should allow other smaller trees to grow faster as there is less competition for nutrients, water, and light. The conditions are favourable for coppicing, and it is expected that with careful management the coppicing could assist the regeneration process. The evidence so far seems to indicate that this is certainly the case. A full forest regeneration cycle is expected every 15 years. Timber extraction is also included in the objectives, but it has a lower medium-term priority. The implementation of the project was divided into five main phases.

(a) Forest inventory. The main objective was to gather sufficient information on the existing volume of wood per hectare, the volume of the different species, wood density, and dbh (breast height diameter).

(b) Evaluation of forest inventory. This was done to determine the type of intervention possible according to the dbh of selected species, in order to estimate the total volume to be cut. It was decided to cut those trees with a diameter of 15 to 30cm at 1.30m above ground. Not all trees within this diameter range are cut, however, because it depends on the density of the trees left standing in a specific location. To meet the minimum required by law, trees within this diameter must be left standing if the minimum tree density is not met. The total standing stock before cutting was estimated to be about 179t/ha, of which an average of 75t/ha is cut – about 40 per cent of the total standing stock. About 30 per cent of the total forest area is left untouched to maintain biological diversity (Cardoso Vale, personal communication).

To determine the potential for regeneration of the forest, the Mean Annual Increment (MAI) of the trees left standing (below 15cm and above 30cm dbh), plus seed-carrying trees are then measured. Certain selected trees are left behind to facilitate regeneration and germination of certain desired species, to ensure a minimum amount of shade in any given exploited area, and to maintain forest density and uniformity. At least 120 trees per hectare of these selected trees are left standing. There are other types of trees which are protected species (such as *Bartoletia excesa* and *Euterpe olerocea*), which must also remain standing as required by law.

(c) Forestry exploration. This is a more complex issue, given the nature of the forests of this region. There are additional difficulties if the number of pioneer trees is very high, as not all of these species are desirable (in this case for charcoal production). Thus the policy is to control unwanted pioneer species and to allow the most suitable ones to flourish. Tree cutting is done in teams of three people: one chainsaw cutter, one assistant, and one other who collects and stacks the wood and ensures that the ground is relatively clean in order to avoid obstructing further exploratory activities, such as the transport of wood. Tree cutters are usually local people who know their trade and cause little damage to other trees when felling. Fallen trees are immediately cut and stacked and then transported to the nearest road or path where the wood is left to dry. Initially, light machinery was used to collect and transport the wood, but the company soon realized that this was causing a lot of damage to the existing forest. In view of this it was decided to use draught animal power (mules and

40

donkeys) to carry the wood out of the forest. In 1992, a new experiment was tried with mechanized harvesting, using short paths in the forest. This did not work, however, and it was decided to return to draught animal power. Wood transportation is costed by the volume transported to a specific location (road or path), usually using three or four mule/donkeys per person; this seems to be more expensive than if machinery is used (Cardoso Vale, personal communication).

(d) Silviculture management. Although fast-growing trees play an important role in the initial regrowth phase, some degree of control is required to prevent undesirable species becoming dominant. Research is being carried out to determine the optimal levels and methods of control to avoid competition with desirable species.

(e) Monitoring. This is a continuous process, essential for the good management of the project, to detect and correct any anomaly at the early stages of regeneration and to improve the economics of sustainable and balanced forestry development. Efforts are being made to develop a continuous monitoring system which would be most suitable for this type of project. Particular attention is being given to soil, rate of revegetation, and climatic characteristics. The hope is to gather sufficient data to develop and proceed with a plan of action. Regeneration capacity has proved to be generally remarkably good, including coppicing from some species that were expected to regenerate through seedling.

There are a number of additional non-forestry problems worth highlighting. Although workers in the charcoal industry are better paid than other unskilled workers, it is still considered a low-prestige activity, making it difficult to recruit personnel in some areas. This difficulty is compounded by the migratory character of the native population of this region of Maranhao, who have little understanding of modern working practices. It is common that after being paid workers will disappear until all their money has been spent before returning to work or will simply move on to other seasonal activities. The problem is further compounded by a lack charcoal-making tradition in this area. All skilled jobs are done by people brought in from outside the region, mainly from MG. Although this situation is now changing, poor education and skills make it very difficult to introduce new technology and to improve productivity. The company hopes that once the population has adapted to the rural milieu this situation will improve. In November 1993 the Fazenda employed about 400 people, a considerable increase on the previous two years.

Given the nature of this type of development and experimentation, operating costs are much higher than in forestry plantations, which are more homogenous and can be mechanically harvested. This is more than compensated for by not having to invest in afforestation.

There is an increased fire hazard with this type of project, because of the lower humidity and the accumulation of residues on the ground. This was tragically demonstrated in December 1991 when a fire destroyed almost 5000ha, most of which was from the area already cut. Although the fire started outside the *fazenda*, it is thought that the residues left behind, together with the drier conditions, played a part. Lessons were learned and measures have been taken to prevent similar accidents happening again, such as ensuring that wood is collected immediately and stacked away from the forest, and making sure that the ground is cleared of the main fire hazards.

The annual charcoal capacity before the 1991 fire was estimated at about 32 000 tonnes per year, but present capacity is about 25 000 tonnes per year. There are two charcoal-making sites, each with a capacity of about 15 000 tonnes per year. Each *carvoaria* is located at the centre of a forest exploitation module of about 250ha which produces, on average, 625 tonnes of charcoal. Once the exploration has been completed, the *carvoaria* moves on to the next exploitation module.

At the moment the only objective is to produce charcoal, but there are other possibilities which may worth exploring, like forest products such as timber, medicinal plants, and fruits, which so far have failed to receive serious attention.

Cosipar, a pig-iron and steel company based in the town of Maraba, is also involved in a similar project of sustainable forest management for charcoal production for its pig-iron works in the Carajas area. They have carried out an analysis which is briefly summarized here. Cosipar is running a project on 23 231ha of forest land. 15 200ha are being managed for sustainable development, and 7400ha as forest reserve in three different locations near Maraba. The company estimates its charcoal demand for 1991–5 to be about 600 000 tonnes, of which 94 500 tonnes are planned to be obtained from sustainable forest development projects. The rest will come either from plantations or forest clearings.

Cosipar is studying how to establish a methodology and socio-economic criteria for the sustainable exploitation of humid tropical forest for large-scale charcoal production, while maintaining the biological diversity of forests. Unlike *Fazenda Descoberta*, Cosipar envisages the cutting of trees with dbh's of between 10 and 50cm. Thus the volume to be cut from the standing stock is much higher, with a cutting cycle every 20 years (Cosipar, 1991). This experiment is still at too early a stage of development to draw any serious conclusions.

In summary, although it is still too early to be able to judge, it seems that sustainable forest management for charcoal production could be a viable economic and environmental alternative to forest destruction. Indeed, the experience of recent years indicates that this is certainly the case. The main obstacle is cost, which is partly caused by unfair competition from illegal cutting activities, lack of a proper tax policy, inefficient sawmills selling their considerable waste very cheaply for charcoal production, and the lack of incentives to SFMPs (Cardoso Vale, personal communication). Charcoal production is not necessarily a 'noble' use of forests, but it may be a major factor in saving them as it increases their economic value considerably. In the short term this remains one of the few viable alternatives for the rational and large-scale exploitation of native forests. It is possible in a worst-case scenario that forests without an economic value will simply disappear.

Doubts still remain as to the capacity and potential of the natural forest to regrow in a short enough cycle to be economically feasible in the long run. But the main problems may be political and institutional rather than economic or technical. Erratic, selective timber extraction has been taking place for many years. It has caused much damage to the forest and it is no longer considered a viable economic or environmentally acceptable alternative.

Given the enormous forestry potential of the region, allied with the high costs of afforestation, there is hope (and self-interest by those who produce and use charcoal) for the sustainable and rational exploitation of the native tropical forests, so that future supplies can be guaranteed. The expansion of steel works, dependent on this type of exploitation, will bring many important additional benefits to the region, such as employment generation, better living standards, and regional socio-economic development in general.

The charcoal-based industrial sector has perhaps a better chance of success in this part of the Amazon than anywhere else in Brazil, given the potential for the sustainable production of charcoal. The region is not suitable for agriculture and cattle ranching because of the poor quality of the soil. In the forest the biological balance is maintained because the diversity allows many species with different requirements for nutrients, water, and soil to survive, thus allowing the forest to flourish. This principle cannot be applied to agricultural and livestock activities.

7. Environmental Factors In Charcoal Production and Use

7.1 General aspects

The iron and metallurgical industry is very polluting and has been subjected to strict environmental and pollution control measures, particularly in industrialized countries. In recent years environmental pressures have increased even further and tougher anti-pollution legislation has been introduced in many countries, forcing the industry to search for less polluting alternatives, mainly through the introduction of anti-pollution equipment. New technological processes are also expected to reduce pollution quite considerably in the future. It is expected that by the year 2000 new processes capable of using coal directly will be widely available in the steel-making industry.

Despite the expected technological advances, coal will continue to form the bulk of raw material for the steel-based industry and hence pollution will continue to be a serious problem. Few developing countries will have the financial resources, and the strong inclination, to use advanced anti-pollution technology.

7.2 Coke versus charcoal

The use of both coke and charcoal in the metallurgical industry presently poses environmental problems and health hazards. It is estimated that in China, about 7000 miners died in mining accidents and coal-related hazards in 1991 alone. But coke is an attractive financial option for the private sector because it allows the productive cycle to be cut dramatically and makes better use of by-products. On environmental, ecological, and social grounds, the balance is in favour of charcoal.

Charcoal production is not without its own environmental problems, as it is often associated with deforestation, partly as a result of the irresponsible behaviour of some sectors of the industry and also because of general misunderstanding. If greater damage has not been caused it is because of the capacity of the natural forest to regrow quickly. There has also been a considerable waste of natural resources, largely the result of disregard for natural forests. Forests were (and still are) often seen as an obstacle to development, particularly among landowners and cattle ranchers. This explains why cleared land can fetch as much as three times the value of forested land. As one environmentalist once put it, 'the desire to get rid of the forests was so great, that the *fazendeiro* did not have time to stop and produce charcoal – fire was quicker!' This is particularly true in the case of the Amazon region, where an estimated 170 000 tonnes of wood are burned daily, enough to produce over 100M tonnes of pig-iron annually – compared with the 0.6M tonnes currently being produced.

If charcoal is produced on a sustainable basis, either from plantations or well-managed native forests, it assumes that all the carbon dioxide liberated during iron-making will be recycled by photosynthesis. Since wood contains little sulphur, charcoal use does not cause acid rain. So in global terms charcoal is much more environmentally friendly than the conventional coke-based route.

Since about 60 per cent of charcoal production is still based on native forests, however, the large-scale use of charcoal in the iron, steel, and metallurgy industries is often questioned because of its perceived negative effects on the environment, particularly with regard to deforestation. This perception is historical, as has already been noted, so it is still common to hear that charcoal production is responsible for large-scale deforestation, particularly in the state of Minas Gerais.

A closer examination, however, shows that it is a more complex issue. There are other states in Brazil which never have had a charcoal industry, such as Para, Sao Paulo, and Santa Catarina, and yet less than 6 per cent of their total land area is covered by native forests today. Even in the Carajas region, by the time the charcoal-based industry was established 38 per cent of the total area was already deforested, and additional large areas suffered from severe degradation. This was the consequence of the expansion of the agricultural frontier and other related activities.

It is important to remember that a large part of the raw material used for charcoal production in Brazil (as much as 96 per cent in the Carajas region) originated from trees and residues from the ever-expanding agricultural, pasture, and timber extraction activities. The charcoal industry has, however, been a source of income for many farmers, and as such helps to finance agricultural expansion and the process of deforestation. Thus in some ways the charcoal industry is an accomplice to this deforestation since it has helped, albeit indirectly, such destruction by providing additional finances to the *fazendeiro* who clears the land of trees.

There is also growing concern about the rapid expansion of plantations, chiefly eucalyptus and particularly on the Atlantic coast, as it is feared that good agricultural land is being used for this purpose. This assumption also seems to be misplaced according to ABRACAVE. In Brazil, millions of hectares of good agricultural land remain idle because of the feudal land tenure system in many parts of the country. The State of MG, for example, has a total area of 58Mha of which, in 1980, 21.5Mha were natural pastures, 18.7Mha *cerrados*, 5.5Mha agricultural land, and just under 2Mha plantations (Neto, 1991). The reason is simple: good agricultural land brings higher returns if used to produce crops rather than forestry plantations. As the study by Abrahao and Furtado (1992) also demonstrates, forest plantations can have a positive socio-economic impact in the local communities.

In general eucalyptus and pine plantations occupy the less productive and poorer soils. Nevertheless, it must be recognized that such plantations are heavily concentrated in some areas. Thus some villages have been described as 'prisoners of eucalyptus', where the local population may have difficulty obtaining land to grow food. Although these may be isolated cases, such situations should certainly be avoided.

Despite such criticism against eucalypts, there is little scientific evidence to prove many of the allegations that eucalyptus contaminates the soil, drains it dry, speeds up desertification, and thrives at the cost of other plants in its vicinity. In 1985, the FAO conducted a detailed study on the possible ecological and environmental effects of eucalyptus. The study concluded that, 'having reviewed the evidence very thoroughly, we must stress that there can be no universal answer, either favourable or unfavourable, to the planting of eucalypts. Nor should there be any answer: each case should be examined on its individual merits. We cannot see how further general research, however, detailed, can alter this conclusion' (Poor and Fries, 1985).

In general, the environmental impacts of eucalyptus plantations are more a consequence of the particular forestry techniques used than the tree species *per se* (Pereira, 1991). Nonetheless, the problem posed by monoculture in general, and eucalypts in particular, are being recognized and greater efforts are being made to diversify, especially using indigenous species. Undoubtedly, charcoal production has some negative environmental impacts. For example, thousands of tonnes of chemicals derived from the charcoal-making process are released intp the atmosphere. This pollution could be significantly reduced with better technology and better use of by-products. This is an area which all main charcoal producers are investigating because of the potential economic implications.

Charcoal-making activities are not more damaging to the environment only because charcoal production generally tends to be a small and dispersed activity, located in rural areas. This causes less environmental damage than would otherwise have been expected, but at the same time makes it more difficult to take full economic advantage of the potential of charcoal, particularly with regard to the use of by-products. It also makes it more difficult to enforce environmental control compared with coke.

It is important to judge any possible environmental impact of charcoal production and use within a wider social, economic, and political context, as these factors are the key to the overall acceptance of charcoal industries. Environmental factors related to charcoal production and use, which are no better or worse than many other similar activities, are not likely to be controlled until Brazilian society as a whole demands greater environmental protection.

7.3 The CO_2 factor

The sustainable exploitation of forests can bring many additional environmental (and economic) benefits. These benefits should be taken into account when comparing the two basic raw materials (charcoal and coke) in the iron, steel, and other related industries.

In the Brazilian forestry plantations sector, there was a total afforested area of about 6Mha in 1990, (over 7Mha in 1995) which would have been responsible for fixing approximately 36M tonnes of carbon per year, (132M tonnes of CO_2); based on a national average productivity of about 12t/ha/yr, and taking into account above ground biomass only. Approximately 2.3Mha of plantation (37 per cent of total) are used for charcoal production, which represents about 13M tonnes of carbon per year, (51M tonnes of CO_2). These estimates should be considered conservative since the estimated productivity can be regarded as low.

Melo et al. (1992) and Rezende et al (1993) estimate that for each tonne of charcoal used (based on pig-iron production) at least 0.4 to 1.2 tonnes of CO_2 (net) is fixed, compared to 1.86 tonnes released by coke-based pig-iron, (see Table 7.1).

In 1992 Brazil produced about 6.2M tonnes of pig-iron using charcoal, of which 39 per cent was based on plantations (ABRACAVE, 1993). Based on the Melo et al (1992) and Rezende et al. (1993) calculations, charcoal-based pig-iron production from plantations would have resulted in at least a net positive balance of about 1M tonnes of CO_2 (6.2 × 0.39 × 0.4) compared to emissions if coke was used. Undoubtedly CO_2 reduction is not the main priority either of the charcoal producers or consumers, but is an additional indirect advantage which has global and national implications.

8. General Perspectives

8.1 General considerations

The charcoal-based industrial sector is at a crossroads. The steel-related industry is going through a difficult and painful period of adjustment to falling demand and overcapacity, both in Brazil and internationally. Strong competition is foreseen in the future as international trading barriers are gradually being reduced. Thus to survive and expand means a need for greater competitiveness and efficiency. To confront these challenges almost every major company has undergone, or is undergoing, a restructuring and modernization process. It is an important challenge to develop new technologies to meet new and tougher environmental controls. This is particularly true with regard to the old coke plants.

In Brazil the steel industry has grown very quickly in the past two and half decades, greatly stimulated by the rapid demand for steel products in the domestic market as well as growing exports. In the future such markets are not expected to grow but to remain stable, except for certain semi-elaborated products such as pig-iron which will be produced mainly for export. This means that greater competition will be inevitable, even in the domestic market, and the closing of less efficient plants will result.

This applies particularly to the charcoal-based sector, where there are many small and inefficient plants still in operation. So far, an important advantage of this sector has been the relatively low cost of charcoal produced (in dollar terms) and the high quality of pig-iron. This is unlikely to continue in the future.

The charcoal-based pig-iron sector has a long tradition in Brazil, but it is not a modern and professionally run industry. In most cases charcoal-making represents an additional income for the *gusero*, who runs his business depending on the price of the pig-iron. If the prices are low the *gusero* quite simply stops production until better times come. The result is that pig-iron sector is particularly undercapitalized (little capital is reinvested), lacks vision and modernization drive, and remains static in this dynamic and intensely capitalized steel-making industry. In many cases it remains an artisan activity rather than a business venture.

Almost the same principle applies to the charcoal production sector from native forests. Far too much charcoal is still being produced from native forest rather than plantations, where old methods, mentalities, and cultural traditions still prevail. Thus the charcoal-based industrial sector faces a big challenge.

(a) Charcoal production. It is clear that present practices cannot continue. Pressure on existing forests, together with social, economic, and environmental considerations, will not permit this situation to continue unchanged for long. Economic efficiency and professionalism will have to be more prominent. Many of the advantages of charcoal from native forests over that from plantations stem from low costs, partly the consequence of illegal activities and avoidance of fiscal responsibilities. These practices will become more difficult in the near future as fiscal pressures will increase.

It is, perhaps, reasonable to think that in order to survive, a smaller sector may be the answer, particularly in MG. Environmental and ecological considerations should be central. Non-renewable supplies of raw materials for charcoal production must be largely confined to the use of forestry residues. On the other hand, it is quite possible that if SFMPs prove successful, the best area of expansion for this type of charcoal manufacturing would be the Eastern Amazon.

(b) Charcoal from plantations. This is the most professionally run sector, but costs remain comparatively high as charcoal production technology has not kept pace with forest management techniques. There are two major problems: (i) the high cost of charcoal and poor use of potential by-products; and (ii) the potential alternative uses of existing plantations, such as pulp and paper, cellulose, furniture, and construction material. At the moment many of these plantations are not suitable for some of these alternative since they were planted for either producing pulp and paper or for charcoal. As these forests are progressively cut, new alternative uses that fetch higher returns will be pursued in preference to charcoal.

(c) Competition with coke. This represents a major challenge for the sector, at least in the short term, as is illustrated by the number of companies who are already planning to start shifting to coke. If the price of coke remains low the decision to use it as a substitute for charcoal will remain popular. The main advantage of coke over charcoal, however, is not necessarily lower direct costs (economic and financial), but the simplification of the production process. Currently, most of the main charcoal producers own large plantations that require large investment in establishment costs, infrastructure, personnel and R&D. This results in high financial costs given the nature of the Brazilian economy and high inflation. By using coke the company eliminates this phase, significantly simplifying the process and therefore making coke an attractive option.

The private sector, mainly concerned with short-term profits and not with social and environmental implications, may be quite willing to put up with the uncertainties associated with possible coke supply problems if there are higher investment returns. Environmental concerns are not a high priority in Brazil. The switch to coke may be an inevitable trend unless charcoal costs can be reduced significantly.

A new tendency is already taking shape. It is possible that even companies which own large plantations may decide to purchase charcoal from third parties rather than produce it themselves, once the present forests have been progressively cut. This will liberate the company of many social responsibilities and allow them to concentrate exclusively on steel making. It is even possible that existing forest plantations could be rented out to third parties and then charcoal would be bought from them. Some of this is already taking place. For example, a number of companies have started to dismantle or reduce their forestry and charcoal R&D facilities, preferring instead to hire such services from third parties.

(d) The pig-iron and steel sector. It is, perhaps, unrealistic to expect the charcoal-based iron and steel industry to survive in its present form. There are far too many small charcoal and pig-iron producers who would not be able to survive the modernization and restructuring process, and the high investment required. Some kind of rationalization process can be expected. In the long term, only the more modern integrated plants are likely to meet the challenge. We think that a number of steps are still needed, and these are briefly described below.

8.2 Research and development needs

The charcoal-based industry is relatively well developed in a number of areas including forest management, infrastructure, and transport. A significant number of improvements have already been made in aspects of forest management such as plant selection, genetic improvement, harvesting techniques, planting and monitoring, and also in the carbonization process, kilns, and charcoal quality (Lima, 1993). Many more improvements are still required, however, ranging from forestry to end products, in order to secure the long-term viability of the industry. The Grupo Itaminas (1989), for example, has estimated that with a minimum investment charcoal consumption per tonne of pig-iron could be reduced by at least 100kg. The Group has estimated that with minor technical improvements charcoal consumption of the Group's plants could be reduced from as much as 800kg of charcoal/tonne of pig-iron in 1989 to about 450–80kg in six years. In some plants of Acesita, for example, the specific consumption of charcoal per tonne of pig-iron has been reduced from 950kg of charcoal/tonne of pig-iron in 1974 to about 575kg in 1992 (Sampaio et al., 1993). It is also possible to substitute up to 20 per cent of charcoal in coke blast furnaces with some minor technical modifications.

Brazil's tradition with charcoal production has sometimes acted as an obstacle to advancement, since the industry has tended to resist new ideas when they have involved additional costs. As Luchi (1987) puts it 'within the Brazilian structure, certain technological practices, once they have established themselves, tend to acquire a permanent character, independently of their techno-economic performance'. Unlike many other industrial sectors, which allowed for the transfer of technology and know-how from other countries, a handicap to the charcoal-based industry has been that the majority of technology and know-how has had to be developed in Brazil. This is because few (if any) countries possess such experience, at least on a large industrial scale.

8.2.1 Forestry

Brazil has extensive experience in forest management, and in many ways it could be considered among the world's leaders in this area. Much research is still required, however, particularly on native species, which has received little attention from the private sector. Research is needed to determine wood density; disease and pest resistance; sprouting and root formation ability; intercropping; nitrogen fixation; selection of better species to meet specific requirements of wood for charcoal-making; biological control programmes; greater attention to environmental matters such as erosion control, water tables and rivers; natural regeneration management; and the development of growth and yield models.

An ambitious long-term R&D programme is currently under consideration in the state of MG, between state research institutions and the private sector, to further develop the charcoal-based industrial sector. This programme includes forestry, charcoal production, by-products recovery, charcoal as a reducing agent, cogeneration of electricity, chemical-based products, new processes, and environmental implications (Furtado et al., 1992). But it remains to be seen if this programme can ever be fully implemented.

8.2.2 Charcoal production

Charcoal-making in Brazil is still an activity which in many ways remains marginal to the mainstream economy. Charcoal is still produced, in most cases, in an almost empirical way in which scientific principles play little part. The personnel involved are often unskilled, which does not facilitate innovative activity. Low pay, together with low status, complicates things even further. Many people in the industry have a sense of backwardness and suffer from low self-esteem.

Thus improvements at almost every level, ranging from social conditions to continuous carbonization technology, and from the use of by-products to improved methods for selecting charcoal sites and the development of a charcoal-chemistry whenever possible, still requires considerable R&D efforts. In addition, the industry should try to diversify its traditional sources of raw materials to new feedstocks such as sugarcane bagasse, straw, and *babassu* residues. These alternatives do not seem to have been fully explored as yet.

Currently, charcoal is produced either from native forests or plantations. In the first case, new environmental protection law enforcement and increased scarcity, particularly in MG, can only result in a short-term option if new alternatives are not found soon. Plantations often have varied end uses which offer greater economic returns than charcoal production; this can cause supply problems unless major improvements in production and use can be made. For example, electricity generation from thermal power plants is becoming increasingly attractive. A number of such plants are being planned (such as CHESF's 30MWe in north-eastern Bahia, and COSIPAR's 12MWe near Maraba, Para). If such plants were successful many more might follow. This could create a supply problem for the charcoal-based industrial sector, and the price of wood would also increase.

8.3 By-products recovery

With modern technologies, charcoal by-products can play a key role in a competitive industry by creating new value-added products.

According to Acesita Energetica, with a modern medium-sized kiln (60t/d of charcoal) the following major by-products could be brought on stream in a short time:

(a) Co-generation of electricity. Direct burning of the gases in the carbonization process could generate 2.5 to 5MW of electricity. This option may be attractive in rural areas which do not have a good supply of electricity.

(b) Production of liquid fuels. This can be achieved through the condensation of gases and steam. The products would be a type of tar oil with a density of about $1.15g/cm^3$, approximately 0.24 tonnes of oil equivalent per tonne of charcoal. The technology is already available but a major difficulty is the low price of tar. Other alternatives may be pursued, such as its use as a fuel oil.

(c) Production of chemicals. During the wood carbonization process, some 600kg of various chemicals are generated for each tonne of charcoal produced. Products which can be obtained from the tar include acetic acid, methanol, acetone, guaiacol, cresol, phenol, 2–6 dimethoxyphenol, and creosote. The main industrial applications are solvents, synthetic fibres, cosmetics, plastics, textiles, resins, and pharmaceuticals. If large industrial quantities of tar were to become available prices would be pushed lower, and hence this alternative may become uneconomic. To become competitive in this market requires considerable effort to develop new and afford-able technological processes for separating and purifying the by-products. This is one of the most promising alternatives, because of its potential added economic value. If all these chemicals were to be separated with maximum theoretical productivity and be commercialized at current prices, the economic value would increase twelve-fold.

Specialty products, such as 2–6 dimethoxyphenol, guaiacol, and cresol, in particular, offer a considerable potential for commercialization given their high prices, although the market is rather small in comparison with the potential offered by the charcoal industry.

Many of these chemical products fetch high prices as fine chemicals, so their large-scale production would have profound implications for the chemical sector. The combination of an expanding market, together with new applications, could be the driving force for charcoal-based chemical products. To give an idea of this potential, Acesita Energetica made preliminary estimates based on a 2000t/d steel plant, using charcoal as a thermo-reducting agent. The annual potential production of charcoal-based products was approximately 100 000t of tars, 42 000t of acetic acid, 10 000t of methanol, 2500t of acetone, and over 4000t of various other products (Acesita Energetica, company information; Sol and Solo, 1986).

Some these of products – methanol, acetone, and acetic acid, are widely used in the chemical industry today and others (cresol, maltol, and 2,6-dimetoxyphenol) are used in both the chemical and pharmaceutical industries. In the short term the most realistic alternative may be to concentrate on the more traditional by-products such as tar, methanol, and acetic acid. The development of new products may prove to be difficult given the present market, financial, and technological limitations.

Acesita Energetica had an extensive R&D programme on charcoal by-products. One of the most important trials was the development of a vertical kiln (retort) for the continuous carbonization of wood (still at the pilot plant stage) with capacity of 15t/day of charcoal and 4t/day of wood tar, installed in Turmalia (MG). The wood is used at a moisture content of 25 per cent, chipped to 30cm, and fed into the top of the kiln. As the wood descends it is heated by a current of gas and steam. The resulting mixture of recycled gasses generated during the carbonization and wood drying process is re-inserted into the tar recuperator and then condensed and stored. The uncondensed materials are reintroduced into the kiln to cool the charcoal and, after condensation, the remainder is used as an energy source. It is generally accepted that any industrial-sized plant must have a capacity three to four times higher (45 to 60t/d charcoal) to be economic. With the privatization of Acesita, however, the future of its R&D programme is very much in doubt. Similar problems apply to other newly privatized companies.

Preliminary studies by Acesita Energetica indicate that the combined production of charcoal and by-products can considerably increase financial returns. For example, in a retort with a capacity of 40t/d that produces charcoal, tar, and ethyl acetate, charcoal represents only 23 per cent of the end-product by value, while 50 per cent of the total value comes from ethyl acetate. The annual return on investment was estimated to be about 32 per cent. In the same retort, producing the same products plus tar, acetic acid, and methanol, the financial return was estimated at 29 per cent; while in a traditional kiln, with tar recovery, the tar would generate 15 per cent annually of the total financial return on investment (Acesita Energetica, company information). Although many of these assumptions should not be regarded as more than an initial evaluation, they show that there is considerable potential for value-added products.

After privatization Acesita Energetica restructured (completed in 1994), a process that will have serious implications for the charcoal sector. At one point the company appeared to have one of Brazil's most advanced R&D programmes on charcoal by-products. Today the research team has been almost disbanded. Some of them, with some financial support from the state government of MG, have set up a private company with the aim of continuing the same line of research. This represents one of the best hopes for continuing research in this area.

Despite all of these difficulties, the charcoal-based industry has many of the ingredients to overcome future developments. A number of alternatives can already be envisaged.

(a) Entrepreneurial vision. Those responsible for running the industry must have vision and self confidence, and run their business professionally and efficiently. The industry has wide socio-economic ramifications in Brazil, particularly in MG, and there are many new opportunities for this industry to modernize and to consolidate. The fact that in the industrialized countries coke has long replaced charcoal has created a certain sense of backwardness and isolation among some professional people in the sector, who believe in the inevitability of coke and see it as siimply a matter of time before charcoal is phased out. This attitude contrasts sharply with that of industrialized countries such as Austria, Sweden, and the USA, where biomass is becoming an important source of energy, particularly for industrial applications. The USA has over 8000MW of biomass electricity and the sector is being boosted by government and utilities.

(b) Modernization. The sector needs to modernize in order to increase productivity and efficiency to compete with coke. This is particularly the case with regard to native forests, where important changes are needed. The use of coke, which already accounts for 65 to 70 per cent, represents at the very least a 'safety valve' for the industry to guard themselves against high charcoal prices. Charcoal has a number of advantages over coke that should be explored to the full, for which most of the technologies are already in place. Clear objectives and determination are needed to speed up the modernization process. Professionalism is possible in the industry as the experience of producing charcoal from forest plantations demonstrates.

(c) Sustainability. It is important to acknowledge sustainability and environmental principles. This is clearly recognized with the 'Fazendeiro

Forestal' programme, and the Sustainable Forestry Management Projects (SFMPs) such as Fazenda Descoberta in the Eastern Amazon. In both cases those involved have shown determination in confronting problems. If the industry does not show vision and determination, it is likely to shrink into insignificance.

There are two main views in Brazil with regard to charcoal:

(a) those who regard the industry as backward, outdated and environmentally damaging. Many environmentalists would be pleased if the industry collapsed, which shows a superficial understanding of the industry, its many socio-economic ramifications, and the real alternatives to charcoal; and

(b) those who see many potential benefits emanating from the charcoal industry. They consider that there is great potential and many opportunities for technological advances that can make the industry financially feasible, sustainable and environmentally friendly. Contrary to what the critics say, there are many opportunities that can bring major socio-economic and environmental gains compared with the current, often inefficient and non-renewable nature of charcoal production. There is also great potential for reducing CO_2 emissions. A successful transition to an efficient fuel-cycle based on forest plantations and SFMP will result in less CO_2 emissions, as is the case of the ethanol programme. If this industry reforms itself, it could represent a major opportunity for greenhouse gas abatement in the country, including the protection of native forests and biodiversity at the same time.

Thus it is important that the charcoal industry put its position across clearly. There many more positive aspects than negative ones. People must be made aware that charcoal can be a catalyst for preserving (not destroying) large areas of native forests if produced renewably; that charcoal can increase the value of the forest and thus help preservation; and that the industry has socio-economic and environmental ramifications which are considerable and not well recognized.

9. Summary and Conclusions

In 1992, about 31 per cent of Brazil's primary energy originated from biomass, equivalent to 47Mtoe (equal to 2.0 EJ and equal to one million barrels of oil a day). Unlike many other developing countries, however, many of these uses are for modern industrial applications. As the world's largest producer of industrial charcoal, Brazil merits particular attention as it has a unique position and experience in the production and use of charcoal.

When opting for charcoal, Brazil took an almost opposite direction to the rest of the world's pig-iron and steel industry. This was a result of a combination of factors, including a lack of indigenous coal, an abundance of iron-ore deposits, extensive forest reserves and land area, and an abundant and cheap labour supply. The introduction of fiscal incentives further stimulated the expansion of commercial plantations. It was the combination of these factors which allowed the country to produce charcoal on such a large scale.

Brazil has gained considerable experience and know-how in forest management, with over 6Mha of commercial plantations, of which about 2.3Mha are dedicated to charcoal production. The rest are for other industrial purposes, particularly pulp and paper. The use of forests on such a large scale, either native or plantations, is bound to cause considerable environmental concern. This study has tried to raise all the main issues concerning charcoal production and use from native and commercial forest plantations in Brazil.

9.1 Charcoal production

Although centuries old, the charcoal-based industrial sector can be regarded as relatively new, since it is almost a post–1945 phenomenon. An important characteristic of the industry, particularly the pig-iron sector, is the large component of small independent producers and its concentration in the sate of Minas Gerais. The small mills found there are the backbone of the industry and are the most vulnerable to the international market fluctuations for pig-iron and steel products, because of their generally low efficiencies.

About 7.3M tonnes of charcoal were produced in 1992. Historically, native forests have provided raw materials for the bulk of charcoal production. This situation is changing, although at a slower pace than

one would like, as more is now being produced from commercial plantations – 39 per cent in 1992, which is expected to continue growing both in
relative and absolute terms.

Minas Gerais is the centre of Brazil's charcoal-based industry. It is a
state deeply committed to charcoal production and is currently debating
whether to implement a large R&D programme to preserve the industry,
following the good examples of FLOREMINAS and Fazendeiro Florestal.
This industry is also a major source of employment with wide socio-
economic ramifications. Charcoal-making and afforestation are labour-
intensive activities, and are often the main source of employment in
many rural communities, particularly among the unskilled and semi-
skilled people who are so numerous in Brazil.

Considerable gains have been made in silvicultural and environmental
matters. For example, different eucalyptus varieties and clones are now
being planted in the same area, allowing greater biological diversity and
the biological control and preservation of about 30 per cent of native
forests.

In most cases charcoal-making can still be considered a craftsman-like
activity in which scientific principles play little or no part. Fortunately this
is changing, particularly among the major and more professional charcoal
producers and consumers. More scientific principles are being applied, with
careful monitoring of wood density, moisture content, and calorific value,
factors hardly considered in the past.

9.2 Charcoal costs

Charcoal costs constitute a major component of the final product manufacturing costs – about 50 to 65 per cent of the cost of pig-iron. In the past
charcoal costs received little consideration, but costs are quite site-specific
and can vary considerably. Prices are often determined by prevailing
market conditions, such as demand for pig-iron and steel products, and
do not necessarily reflect real production costs, as stated in chapter 5.

The relatively high cost of charcoal in Brazil, despite low wages, is a
result of a number of factors, such as high transport costs and low
production efficiencies. These costs need to be reduced in real terms if
charcoal is to compete with coke, which is increasingly becoming an
attractive alternative to charcoal.

The aggressive pursuit of by-products can play a significant role in
making the industry more competitive and modern, at least in the medium
and long term, although market conditions and know-how may be major
determinants. Furthermore, by-products offer a considerable potential and
are an option which the industry should pursue more vigorously. The co-
generation of electricity, together with the production of some liquid fuels
and chemical products, looks particularly promising.

9.3 Sustainable Forestry Management Projects (SFMPs)

A central theme of this book has been the need for environmentally and ecologically sustainable production and use of charcoal, either from native forests or commercial plantations. Surely this is a major challenge of the future.

In section 6.2 we examined in some detail a specific example of SFMP, that of 'Fazenda Descoberta' in the Carajas region. It is a good example of charcoal production from humid tropical forests on a sustainable and rational basis. Although it is not yet a proven system, if successful, it could form the basis for preserving large areas of native forests. It is encouraging that other companies operating in Carajas now recognize this potential.

The best guarantee of survival for the tropical natural forest is to find an alternative economic value, something which is generally lacking at the moment. There is a large forestry potential in the Amazon which is far from being realized.

SFMP projects appear to be an economically and environmentally viable alternative, at least under present circumstances. Charcoal production is not necessarily the most noble use of forests, but it may be one of the best alternatives for large-scale exploitation and preservation of the native Amazon forests. Much will depend, however, on human intervention and

Eucalyptus can be interplanted with other species, and can be used for animal grazing.

the capability of the Amazon forests to regenerate in order to guarantee the economic viability of SFMP.

9.4 Environment

Three major environmental concerns have arisen with regard to large- scale charcoal production. The first concerns the potential destruction of natural vegetation. In Brazil, however, the main responsibility for large-scale deforestation has not been the charcoal industry, but the expansion of agricultural and grazing land. Charcoal from native forests has largely been produced from forest clearings. For example, in the Carajas region as much as 96 per cent of raw material originates from sawmill residues, forestry, and agricultural activities.

There are also environmental concerns posed by large eucalyptus plantations. Four main objections have arisen in recent years:

(a) The heavy concentration of plantations in some areas, particularly in the state of MG. Some of these areas have been described as 'prisoners of eucalyptus'. Though these may be isolated cases, such situations should be avoided.

(b) Concern is growing that eucalyptus plantations use good agricultural land. Again this may be the case in certain areas, but generally this is not supported by the facts. In MG, for example, eucalyptus plantations are found mostly on poorer soils which have been degraded and are often unsuitable for agriculture.

(c) The third objection concerns eucalyptus itself. There have been many allegations that *Eucalyptus spp.* contaminates the soil, drains it dry, and thrives at the expense of other plants in the vicinity. There is little scientific evidence to support this view. In general, the environmental impacts of eucalyptus plantations are no better or worse than other similar species. Any environmental impact is more a consequence of the particular forestry techniques used than the tree species *per se*.

(d) Finally, is the concern with the loss of biological diversity in plantations compared with natural forests. Large plantations, by their nature, undoubtedly cause some loss of biological diversity. Important lessons have been learned early in Brazil, however, and such plantations are now being used to improve local diversity by rehabilitating degraded land with poor diversity resulting from annual burning, erosion, or overgrazing. Rehabilitation is partly done by afforestation with different species and clones of Eucalyptus, interplanting them with other species, and by leaving about one-third of the land area to natural regeneration throughout to enhance diversity.

The third major environmental concern refers to charcoal-making activities. Charcoal production undoubtedly has certain negative environmental impacts. Today thousands of tonnes of chemicals derived from the charcoal-making processes are released into the atmosphere. This pollution could largely be reduced with better technology and better use of by-products. Generally, however, this activity is not a serious environmental hazard as it is a widely disperse activity, away from population centres.

On the other hand there are very clear environmental advantages of the charcoal-based industry, as it produces little sulphur or nitrous oxides and overall it does not contribute CO_2. With all its defects charcoal is still far more environmentally friendly than coke, as discussed in sections 4.2 and 8.1.

In the end one must try to strike a balance between one's beliefs and what is realistically achievable. 'Environment' means different things to different people. While in industrialized countries environmental matters are usually a key component of socio-economic policy, this is not necessarily the case in developing countries where poverty, unemployment, and lack of running water, among other factors, are more pressing priorities. Brazil is no exception to this case.

It must be accepted that the charcoal-based industry has made considerable advances in recent years, notably in forest management, infrastructure, transport, and mechanization, although much remains to be done. Generally, the industry needs to be modernized and to have a more positive attitude to innovation, and to invest in R&D, if it is to have a secure future. Many production, consumption and end- use areas still require considerable R&D efforts to improve efficiency at almost every level. The industry must also consider other raw materials for charcoal production, such as sugarcane bagasse, straw, and babassu shells.

10. References

ABRACAVE, *Anuarios Estadisticos*. (ABRACAVE – Associacao Brasileira de Carvao Vegetal), Belo Horizonte, MG, 1990, 1991, 1992, 1993.

ABRACAVE, 'Polo Forestal de Minas Gerais'. ABRACAVE, Belo Horizonte, MG, 1993a. (unpublished document)

Abrahao, J. and Furtado D.B., *A Acesita Energetica no Alto Jequitinhonha*. Acesita Energetica, Belo Horizonte, MG, 1992.

Acesita, *Modernizacao da Producao de Carvao Vegetal*. Acesita S/A, Belo Horizonte, MG, 1991.

Acesita Energetica, (Company Information), Belo Horizonte, MG.

Ackerman, F. and Almeida, P.E.F., 'Iron and Charcoal: The industrial fuelwood crisis in Minas Gerais'. *Energy Policy*, 1990, pp.661–8.

Andrade, E.N., *O Eucalipto*. Cia Paulista de Estradas de Ferro, Jundiai, SP, 1961.

ANON, *Assessoria Tecnica e Projetos de Manejo Florestal Sustentado*. Del Rey Servicos de Engenharia Ltda, Belo Horizonte, MG, 1989.

ASICA, *Forestry Plan for Sustainable Carajas Pig Iron Industry*. Associacao das Siderurgicas de Carajas, Belo Horizonte, MG, 1991.

ANFPC, *O Setor de Papel e Celulose em 1992*. ANFPC: Associacao Nacional dos Fabricantes de Papel e Celulose, Sao Paulo, SP, 1993.

Assis, P.S., Marinho, L.Z., and Porto, F.M. 'Utilizacao do Carvao Vegetal na Siderurgia'. Mannesmann, Belo Horizonte, MG. 1982. (unpublished report)

Barros, N.F. and Novias, R.F., (eds), *Relacao Solo-Eucalipto*. Departamento de Solos, Centro de Ciencias Agrarias, Universidade Federal de Vicosa, MG, 1990.

Belo Elian, J.M. *Personal communication*. Industrial Director, Companhia Siderurgica Vale do Pindare, Belo Horizonte, MG, 1993.

BEN, *Balanco Energetico Nacional 1993* (National Energy Balance). Ministry of Mines and Energy, Brasilia, Brazil, 1993.

Betters, D.R., Wright, L.L., and Cuotos, L. 'Short Rotation Woody Crop Plantations in Brazil and the United States'. *Biomass and Bioenergy*, 1, 1992, pp.305–16.

Bialy, J., *A New Approach to Domestic Fuelwood Conservation: Guidelines for Research*. FAO, Rome, 1986.

de Bovet, A., *A Industria Minera na Provincia de Minas Gerais*. Annaes de Escola de Minas de Ouro Preto, No.2 (Ouro Preto), 1883. (Quoted in OSSE 1982).

Brito, J.O., 'Principios de Producao e Utilizacao de Carvao Vegetal de Madeira', *Documentos Florestais* 9, University of Sao Paulo, Piracicaba, SP, Brazil, 1990.

Brito, J.O., 'Forest as Energy Source in Brazil', Departamento das Ciencias

Florestais, ESALQ, University of Sao Paulo, Piracicaba, SP, Brazil, 1991.

Caixeta, A.F. and Braga, R.N.B.A., *Siderurgia Integrada a Carvao Vegetal*. Belgo Mineira, Belo Horizonte, MG, 1993.

Campos, T.L. and Toninello, S.L., 'Condicoes de Financiamento de Florestas para Producao de Carvao'. 40 Encontro Tecnico Florestal/ABRACAVE, Belo Horizonte, MG, 1989.

Cardoso Vale, L.C. and Nascimento, M.B.,'Projecao das Necesidades de Plantio e Investimentos para o Setor Siderurgico a Carvao Vegetal 1989–2000'. 40 Encontro Tecnico Florestal/ABRACAVE, Belo Horizonte, MG, 1989.

Cardoso Vale, L.C., *Personal communication*. Del Rey Servicios de Engenharia Ltda, Belo Horizonte, MG, 1991 and 1993.

CEMIG, *8 Balanco Energetico Estadual* (8th Energy Balance of the State of MG). CEMIG: Companhia Energetica de MG, Belo Horizonte, MG, 1993.

COSIPAR, Companhia Siderurgica do Para, (Company Information). Maraba, Para, 1991.

CVRD, *Cenarios do Mercado Internacional de Gusa no Ano 2000*, Company Information, Belo Horizonte, MG, (Companhia Vale do Rio Doce), 1992.

Delfino N., *Producao de Carvao Vegetal na Regiao da Estrada de Ferro Carajas*. Florestas Rio Doce, SA, Belo Horizonte, MG, 1984.

Book of Vital Statistics: A Complete Guide to the World Figures. The Economist/Hutchinson, London, 1990.

Emrich, W., *Handbook of Charcoal-making*. D. Reidel Publishing Co., (Series E: Energy from Biomass, Vol.7), Dordrecht, 1985.

Evans, J., *Plantation Forestry in the Tropics* (2nd edn). Clarendon Press, Oxford, 1992.

Evans, J. 'Forest Resources Assessment 1990: Tropical countries', *FAO Forestry Paper 112*. FAO, Rome, 1993.

'Industrial Charcoal-making', *FAO Forestry Paper 63*. FAO, Rome, 1985.

Fearnside, P.M., and Rankin, J.M., 'Jari and Development in the Brazilian Amazon', *Interciencia*, 1980, Vol.5, pp.146–56.

Fearnside, P.M. and Rankin, J.M., 'Jari Revisited: Changes and the Outlook for Sustainability in the Amazon's Largest Silvicultural Estate', *Interciencia*, 1985, Vol.10, pp.121–9.

Fearnside, P.M., 'Jari at Age 19: Lessons for Brazil's Silvicultural Plants at Carajas's', *Interciencia*, 1988, Vol.13, pp.13–24.

Ferreira, M., A Situacao Florestal Brasileira e o Papel da Silvicultura Intensiva, *Documentos Florestais*, 1989, Vol.2. University of Sao Paulo, ESALQ, Piracicaba, SP, Brazil.

Ferreira, A.C., *Personal communication*. Technical Co-ordinator, Acesita Energetica, Belo Horizonte, MG, 1991.

Filho, M.B.N., Cardoso Vale, L.C., and Assis, S.L. 'Plano de Manejo Sustentado – COSIPAR. Companhia Siderurgica do Para, Maraba, Para, 1990.

Foley, G., *Charcoal-making in Developing Countries: Technical Report No.5.* Earthscan, London, 1986

Freitas, G.D., de Oliveira, A.C., and Hahne, H., 'Tutoramento Ambiantal na Mannesmann Fi-EL Florestal'. 2nd Annual Seminar on Environmental Impacts, Espinho, Portugal, 29 March – 7 April, 1992.

Furtado, P. *Personal communication.* Chief, Energy Division, Fundacao Centro Tecnologico de Minas Gerais, Belo Horizonte, MG, 1992 and 1993.

Furtado, P., Ayres, A.P., and Figueira, R.M., 'Programa de Pesquisa e Desenvolvimento em Biomassa e Siderurgia a Carvao Vegetal-Descricao Geral'. CETEC, Belo Horizonte, MG, 1992.

Grandin, F.H., Gudenau, H.W., Assis, P.S., and Birkhauser, L. 'Charcoal – Injection into a Charcoal Blast Furnace: Combustion Properties in the Raceway'. 2nd European Ironmaking Congress, 15–18 September, Glasgow, UK, 1991.

GRUPO ITAMINAS, Technical Development, 'Charcoal Consumption Decrease Blast Furnace for Pig Iron Production' (unpublished report), 1989.

GRUPO ITAMINAS, 'Projeto Reflorestamento para Producao Siderurgica na Amazonia Oriental'. (Programa Polos Florestais na Amazonia), Belo Horizonte, MG, 1991.

Heinisch, R.S., 'Meio Ambiente: Siderurgia a Carvao Vegetal e Coke, Divisao de Meio Ambiente'. Acesita S/A, Belo Horizonte, MG, 1991.

Hollingdale, A.C., Krishnan, R., and Robinson, A.P., *Charcoal Production: A Handbook.* CSC (91) ENP–27 Technical Paper 268. Natural Resources Council and Commonwealth Science Council, London, 1991.

IBAMA, 'Statistical Data'. Instituto Brasileiro de Meio Ambiente, Belo Horizonte, MG, 1991.

IBDF, 'Estadisticas de Reflorestamento'. IBDF (Instituto Brasileiro de Desenvolvimento Florestal), Brasilia, DF, 1988.

Instituto Brasileiro de Siderurgia (IBS), Vol.35/36, Rio de Janeiro, RJ, 1980.

de Jesus, R.M.,'The Need for Reforestation'. Paper presented at the Workshop on Large-Scale Reforestation, Corvallis, Oregon, USA (organized by the US Environmental Protection Agency), 1993.

Johansson, T.B.J., Kelly, H., Reddy, A.K.N., and Williams, R.H., 'Renewable Fuels and Electricity for a Growing World Economy', in Chapter 1, *Renewables for Fuels and Electricity,* eds T.B.J. Johansson et al. Island Press, Washington DC, 1993.

Juvillar, J.B., and Nogueira, C.P.,' Secagem ao Ar da Madeira de Eucalipto para Producir Carvao Siderurgico', 43 Congresso Anual–88. Associacao Brasileira de Metais, SP, pp.291–310.

Lei Florestal, *Lei Florestal de Minas Gerais.* Lei 10561 (27 December 1991). Decreto de Regulamento, Instituto Estadual de Florestas, Belo Horizonte, MG, 1991.

Lima, W.P.,'Impacto Ambiental do Eucalipto'. EdUSP, Sao Paulo, SP, 1993.

Luchi, N.R., 'Consideracoes sobre Modelos para Producao de Carvao

Vegetal na Regiao de Carajas'. Paper presented at the seminar Floresta e Siderurgia: A Experiencia de Minas Gerais e Perspectivas para a Amazonia, held in Sao Luis de Maranhao, MA, Brazil. Natron – Consultoria e Projetos, 1987.

Macedo, P., *Personal Communication.* Consultant, Belo Horizonte, MG, 1993 and 1994.

Melo, M.C.F., Oliveira, S.P., Rezende, M.E.A., and Sampaio, R.S. 'Self-Sustained Ironmaking and the Environmental Issue'. Companhia Acos Especiais Itabira, Belo Horizonte, MG, 1992.

Moreira, J.R., Serra, G.E., and Trindade, S., *Alternative Liquid Fuels.* Wiley Eastern Ltd., Delhi, and UN University Press, Tokyo, 1992.

Neto, J.L.M. 'Siderurgia a Carvao Vegetal: Um Dilema Emocional'. ABRACAVE, Belo Horizonte, MG, 1991.

Neto, J.L.M., *Personal communication.* President-Director, CAF – Cia Agricola e Florestal Santa Barbara, Belo Horizonte, MG, 1993.

Nogueira, C.P. and Oliveira, A.C., 'Bioenergia para Siderurgia, Mannesmann FI-El Florestal'. Belo Horizonte, MG, 1991.

Nogueira, C.P., Oliveira, A.C., and Hahne, H., 'Forno de Alveria Rectangular para Carbonizacao de Eucalipto'. Mannesmann Fi-El Florestal, Belo Horizonte, MG., 1991. (unpublished)

Nooten, F., and Raymaekers, V., 'Early Iron Smelting in Central Africa', *Scientific American,* 1988, 259(1) p.84.

Openshaw, K., 'Measuring Fuelwood and Charcoal' in *Wood Fuel Surveys.* FAO, Rome, 1983, pp.173–8.

Osse, L., 'Consumo de Carvao Vegetal e Atividades Florestais da Siderurgia Brasileira – Recapitulacao Cronologica'. Companhia Agricola e Florestal Santa Barbara, Belo Horizonte, MG, 1982. (unpublished)

Panday, D., *Assessment of Tropical Forest Plantation Resources.* Swedish University of Agricultural Sciences, Department of Forest Surveys, Uppsala, Sweden, 1992.

Poor, D., and Fries, 'Ecological Effects of Eucalyptus', *FAO Forestry Paper 59.* FAO, Rome, 1985.

Pereira, J.S., 'Environmental Impact Assessment in Afforestation with Eucalyptus in Portugal', in *EC Workshop on Afforestation of Agricultural Land.* EC, Brussels, December 1991.

Rezende, M.E.A., 'Modernizacao da Producao de Carvao Vegetal – Carbonizacao Continua'. Acesita S/A, Belo Horizonte, MG, (undated). (unpublished)

Rezende, J.L.P., Vale, A.B., and Minette, L.J., 'Estudo Comparativo dos Custos de Producao de Carvao da Madeira da Vegetacao Nativa e de Eucalyptus Spp.', in *Arvore,* 1987, Vol.11(1), pp.90–104.

Rezende, G.C., and Cardoso, J.M., 'Analise Economica para Contratacao de Servicos Florestais'. 4o. Encontro Tecnico Florestal/ABRACAVE, Belo Horizonte, MG, 1989.

Rezende M.E.A., Lessa, A., Pasa, V., Sampaio, R., and Macedo, P., *Commercial Charcoal Manufacture in Brazil.* First Biomass Energy Congress of the Americas: Energy, Environment, Agriculture, and

Industry. Burlington, Vermont, USA, NREL, Golden, Co. 80401 Vol.II, 1993, pp.1456–71.

Rezende, M.E.A., Capanema, F.M., Oliveira, S.P., amd Sampaio, R.S., *Self-Sustainable Ironmaking – The rebirth of an Earth Friendly Process*. 7th European Conference on Biomass for Energy and the Environment, Agriculture, and Industry. D.O. Hall, G. Grassi, and H. Scheer, (eds). Ponte Press, Bochum, 1994, pp.490–7.

Rivelli, J.G., and Rezende, M.E.A., *Charcoal Production from Planted Forests: A Brazilian Experience*. 1st Workshop of the FAO/CNRE on Charcoal and Production and Pyrolysis Technologies, Roeros, Norway, 1989.

Rodriguez, L.C.E.,'Topicos de Economia Florestal', in *Documentos Florestais*, Vol.12, 1991, University of Sao Paulo, ESALQ, Piracicaba, SP.

Sampaio, R.S., Chevrand, L.J.S., Fhilo, F.B., Martins, T.B., Fonseca, M.A.P., Oliveira, S.P., *The Use of Self-Sustainable Pig-Iron in the EAF*. Proceedings of 16th Advanced Technology Symposium – Alternate Iron Sources for the EAF, Myrtle Beach, South Carolina, Iron Steel Society, 1993.

Schubert, H.R., *History of the British Iron and Steel Industry*. Routledge and Keagan Paul, London, 1957.

Sena, J.C.D., *Viagem de Estudos Metalurgicos no Centro de Provincia de Mina*. Annaes da Escola de Minas de Ouro Preto, No.1, Rio de Janeiro, 1981. (Quoted in Osse, 1982)

SINDER, 'Sindicato da Industria do Ferro'. SINDER, Belo Horizonte, MG, 1993.

Sociedade de Investigacoes Florestais (SIF), *Estudo de Viabilidede da Implantacao e Reforma de Macicos Florestais para Fins Energeticos com Eucalyptus*. Universidade Federal de Vicosa, Vicosa, MG, 1986.

SOL and SOLO, *Carboquimica Vegetal*, No.13. Belo Horizonte, MG, 1986.

Trossero, M.A., 'Evaluation of Charcoal-making Technologies in Developing Countries', in *Charcoal Production and Pyrolysis Technologies*. FAO/REUR Technical Series 20, Rome, 1991, pp.18–29.

Valente, O.F., Ladeira, A.M.M., Vital, B.R., Ladeira, H.P., 'O Estado da Arte da Producao de Carvao Vegetal'. Universidade de Vicosa, Centro de Ciencias Agrarias, Vicosa, MG, 1991. (unpublished)

Verissimo, A., Barreto, P., Matos, M., Tarifa, R., and Uhl, C., 'Logging Impacts and Prospects for Sustainable Forest Management in an Old Amazonian Frontier: The Case Of Paragominas', *Forest Ecology and Management*, Vol.55, 1992, pp.169–99.

Tables

Table 1.1 Evolution of charcoal consumption in the main industrial sectors in Brazil, 1978–91. (10³t)

Year	Charcoal from native forests	%	Charcoal from planted forests	%1	Total
1978	3 330	88	458	12	3 788
1979	3 779	87	546	13	4 324
1980	4 216	85	694	15	4 910
1981	3 939	81	914	19	4 853
1982	3 732	80	933	20	4 665
1983	4 606	82	1 202	18	5 808
1984	6 150	83	1 253	17	7 403
1985	6 521	63	1 375	37	7 896
1986	7 263	82	1 516	18	8 779
1987	6 949	81	1 656	19	8 605
1988	7 141	78	2 014	22	9 155
1989	7 975	71	3 226	29	11 201
1990	6 089	66	3 137	34	9 226
1991	4 469	58	3 276	42	11 020
1992	4 456	61	2 838	39	7 294

Source: ABRACAVE, 1990, 1991, 1993

(1) Decree No.97.628 (12/4/89) required that the percentage of charcoal to be obtained from plantations must be as follows: 1989 = 40 per cent; 1990 = 50 per cent; 1995 = 100 per cent. The same decree allows to 20 per cent of charcoal to be produced from forest residues and hence in actual practice the macimm amount of charcoal to be produced from plantations would not be over 80 per cent of total, as from 1995 onwards.

Table 2.1 Classification of the Brazilian pig-iron and steel industry by group in 1992.

Sector	Product. (Mt/year)	Coke and charcoal consumpt. (Mt/year)	Number of companies
Coke-integrated steel	16.70	8.90	5
Semi-integrated steel	2.70	–	20
Charcoal integrated steel	3.98	1.68	8
Charcoal independent pig-iron	4.38	5.20	78
Charcoal ferro-alloys	0.98	0.73	23

Source: ABRACAVE (1993); SINDER (1993)

Table 2.2 Industrial consumption of charcoal in Brazil, 1988–92. (10^3t charcoal)

Group	1988	1989	Year 1990	1991	1992
Steel-integrated plants	2 825	2 925	2 100	1 950	1 675
Pig-iron (independent producers)	4 100	5 325	4 650	3 725	3 500
Ferro-alloys	850	1 025	775	750	725
Cement	775	625	550	375	325
Metallurgy (primary metals)	325	400	400	325	300
Others	300	900	725	600	750
Total	9 175	11 200	9 200	7 725	7 275

Source: ABRACAVE, (1991) and (1993)

Table 3.1 Afforestation with fiscal incentives in Brazil, 1967–86. (1000ha)

Year	Pinus	Eucalyptus	Other	Total
1967	18	14	3	35
1968	61	30	12	103
1969	96	54	12	162
1970	120	84	18	222
1971	99	129	21	249
1972	101	172	31	304
1973	86	161	47	294
1974	83	188	53	324
1975	94	223	81	398
1976	87	262	100	449
1977	99	194	53	346
1978	141	228	43	412
1979	118	283	73	474
1980	89	272	75	436
1981	117	230	71	418
1982	158	187	86	431
1983	74	91	50	215
1984	71	124	91	286
1985	65	131	89	285
1986	85	174	150	409
TOTAL	1 862	3 231	1 159	6 252

Source: IBDF (1988), Estadisticas de Reflorestamento, Brasilia, DF; Jesus (1990)

(The total afforestation area in 1993 is estimated to be about 6.5Mha.)

Table 3.2 Afforested area by small and medium-scale farmers programme: Fazendeiro Florestal, MG. (in ha)

Associated Members of ABRACAVE	1989	1990	1991	1992
	6 325	7 680	3 463	6 618
Non-members of ABRACAVE	3 034	4 698	4 513	6 626
Total	9 349	12 378	7 976	13 244

Source: ABRACAVE (1993)

Table 3.3 Employment in the charcoal-based industries, 1989 and 1992.

Area	Year 1989	1992	Observations
1) Afforestation	51 358	44 300	Planting, harvesting, maintenance, transport
2) Charcoal from native forests	134 600	75 200	Harvest, transport of charcoal
3) Integrated steel production	467 72	33 800	Direct employment by steel industry
4) Pig-iron	22 608	16 200	Direct employment by steel industry
5) Ferroalloys	12 000	10 700	Direct employment by steel industry
Total	267 438	180 200	

Source: ABRACAVE, (1990), (1991), (1992)

Table 4.1 Main characteristics of a typical industrial charcoal kiln.

Kiln diameter (base)	5m	
Nominal kiln volume (wood)		$22–27m^3$ (5.4–6.6t) (1)
Operating cycle		
Loading		4 hrs (2 men)
Unloading		5 hrs (2 men)
Carbonization		96 hrs
Cooling		96 hrs
Yield		
Charcoal (db)		33 per cent (in weight)
Volumetric conversion efficiency		
Rate per $1m^3$ (2)	$1–1.2m^3$.(1.8–2 steres)	
Wood humidity		25–30 per cent
Charcoal production efficiency		$1–1.4.m^3$/ha/yr
Useful life of kiln		4 years
Annual charcoal production (appx)		5 400m^3 (about 1350kg)
Volumetric efficiency of charcoal per tonne of pig iron	$1– 0.8t$ (4.2–3.2 m^3) (3)	

Notes:

(1) Charcoal is measured either in m^3 or steres, both of which can vary considerably but generally $1m^3$ = 1.66 steres. This ratio varies in practice according to the type of wood, e.g. one stere of dry eucalyptus wood is about $0.6m^3$, although this is not always the case. Usually one tonne contains $4m^3$ but this also tends to vary and $3.7m^3$ per tonne is also used. Here, unless otherwise indicated, $1t = 4m^3$.

(2) The volumetric conversion efficiency rate varies considerably depending on the type of kiln, management, wood characteristics etc. Efficiencies of $1.3–0.96m^3$ (2.2 – 1.6 steres) of charcoal are also common.

(3) Volumetric efficiency of charcoal to pig-iron depends on many factors including charcoal quality (eg. density to the type of the pig-iron kiln). In the most modern kilns efficiencies of up to $2.6m^3$/charcoal (650kg) per one tonne of pig iron have been achieved. In the future an efficiency of $1.9m^3$ (475kg) of charcoal (and even better) can be expected to be achieved. Wood density is also an important factor. This can vary from 230 to 250kg/m^3 in the cerrado area (native forests), and 270 to 280kg/m^3 in the Carajas region, to less than 200kg/m^3 for the eucalyptus plantations.

Sources: Rivelli Rezende (1989); Neto (1991); Grupo Itaminas (1989); Furtado (1993)

Table 4.2 Main characteristics of charcoal and coke.

	Charcoal		Coke
A) Properties			
Chemical:			
Fixed carbon	70–75%		85–90%
Ash	3–5		8–10%
Volatiles	20–25	<01%	
Moisture	5–35		3–7%
Sulphur	003–006		0.5–1%
Physical:			
Strength	18.3 (% >25.4mm)		55.1 (% >25.4mm)
Grainsize	15–100 (mm)		30–00 (mm)
Density	200–280 (kg/cbm)		450–500 (kg/cbm)
Metallurgical:			
Boudouard temp.	750–800°C		950–1000°C
B) General characteristics			
Origin	wood		coal
Average specific weight	250kg/m^3		500kg/m^3
Average calorific value	7000kcal/kg		6900kcal/kg
Ratio wood to charcoal	1.8 stere/m^3		–
Nature of raw material	renewable		non-renewable
C) Main characteristics when used in blast furnaces			
Calorific value of gas	900kcal/nm^3		800kcal/nm^3
Average content of carbon	460kg/t pig-iron		420kg/t pig-iron
Fraction of fines	25%		10%
Productivity (total vol.)	1.80t/m^3		2.2t/m^3
Average consumption to charcoal-raw cake	3.2m^3/t pig-iron 780kg/t pig-iron		500 kg/t p.i
Iron slag	200kg/t pig-iron		300kg/t pig-iron
Average cost (factory)	$30–31/m^3		$247*/t
D) Main characteristics of pig-iron process in kilns			
Volume	<		>
Height	<		>
Pig-iron temperature	1400°C		1550°C
Desulphurization	unnecessary		required
Residues	dangerous		dangerous

Sources: (a) Grandin et al. (1991); (b,c,d) Heinisch (1990); Acesita Energetica (company information);
* Ferreira, (1991)
Stere – see Table 4.1

Table 4.3 Main characteristics of charcoal for blast furnaces of Belgo-Mineira, MG, Brazil.

Chemical and Physical composition of charcoal (dry basis – by weight	Range		Yearly	Charcoal
	Max.	Min.	Average	Good to Excellent
Carbon	80%	60%	70%	75–80%
Ash	10%	3%	5%	3–4%
Volatile matter	26%	15%	25%	20–25%
Bulk density (kgs/m³)	330	200	260	250–300
Bulk density (dry)	270	180	235	230–270
Average size (mm)	60	10	35	20–50
Fines content (–6.35mm)	22%	10%	15%	10% Max
Moisture content	25%	10%	10%	10% Max

Note: Good to excellent charcoal denotes charcoal produced from Belgo Mineira's own eucalyptus plantations.

Source: Trossero (1991)

Table 5.1 Average charcoal prices in Brazil for 1992 and 1982–92 (at constant US$).

	Year			
	1992		1982–1992	
	$/m³	$/tonne	$/m³	$/tonne*
Minas Gerais	14.9	59.6	16.2	65.0
Sao Paulo	16.0	63.6	15.1	61.6
Rio de Janeiro	15.0	60.0	16.8	67.5
Bahia	14.5	58.0	16.0	64.0
Espiritu Santo	14.6	58.5	15.0	60.0
Brazil	15.0	60.0	15.8	63.6

Note:

* Figures have been rounded.

Source: ABRACAVE, 1993

Table 5.2 Estimated approximate cost of charcoal from well-managed forests, in Minas Gerais.

	$/m^3$
1) Wood Costs	
Standing green matter	4.36
Air dried	5.13
Wood cost (in terms of charcoal volume) (1)	9.00
2) Harvest Costs (stere)	
Cutting (air dried)	1.41
Wood preparation for loading	0.17
Loading/unloading of wood	0.77
Transportation to kiln-site (2)	0.034
Other internal transport costs	0.45
Administrative costs	2.41
Harvest cost + administrative cost (3)	5.24
3) Harvest costs (based on charcoal volume) (3)	9.50
4) Carbonization costs	5.80
5) Average transport costs (4)	3.80
Total Costs (factory gate) (5)	28.00*

Notes:
(1) Conversion rate = 1.8 stere per m^3, less 15 per cent volume reduction
(2) Transport distance = 10km
(3) Conversion rate 1.8 stere = $1m^3$
(4) Average transport distance = 304km
(5) Includes 5 per cent loss during charcoal transportation
* Rounded figure.

Source: Furtado (1992)

Table 5.3 Summary of estimated cost of charcoal from Amazon forests on a non-sustainable basis (1984$/m³).

Item	Paragominas	nr. Maraba
Infrastructure	0.71	1.06
Wood cutting/chipping	3.10	4.14
Carbonization process	0.99	2.51
Administration	0.52	1.10
Personnel (recruitment and (transport)	–	0.50
Others	–	1.54
Sub-total	5.62	10.86
Transport of Charcoal		
50km	–	2.11
120km	–	3.39
240km	–	4.41
280km	4.57	–
Total costs		
50 km	–	12.97
120 km	–	14.25
240 km	–	15.27
280 km	10.19	–
Total costs of factory gate		
50 km	–	13.00
120 km	–	14.28
240 km	–	15.30
280 km	10.19	–
Charcoal price (factory gate)	11.14	–
Profit	0.94	

* Exchange rate July 12, 1984 – US$1 = CR$1,961

Source: Compiled from Delfino (1984) and Florestas Vale Rio Dace (Company information)

Table 5.4 Summary of costs of charcoal production from sustainable forestry management project, Fazenda Descoberta.

	$/t charcoal[1]
Operational Exploration (cutting, cleaning, etc)	22
Transport cost of wood to kiln-site	20
Carbonization process	10
Transport to plant	12
Other (taxes, capital depreciation, etc)	13
Total	$77/t ($19.25/m^3)*

Notes
1. 1t of wood = 250kg of charcoal

* By November 1993, direct cost of charcoal production were reduced in most instances to about $53/t ($14/m^3).

Price of pig-iron:
Domestic market 90 per cent = $140/t
Export markets 10 per cent = $130/t
(In December 1991 the price of pig-iron fluctuated around $100/t).
Cost of charcoal 1m^3 = $19.25. (The price includes only exploration, carbonization, and transport to pig-iron plant; excludes costs associated forest maintenance).

Source: Cardoso Vale (1993); Belo Elian (1993)

Table 7.1 Summary of CO$_2$ balance from charcoal and coke-based pig-iron production (kg per tonne of pig-iron).

Process	Release of CO$_2$	
	Charcoal	Coke
Carbonization	1 496	160
Sintering	144	114
Reduction agent	1 791	1 589
Sub-total	3 431	1 863
Photosynthesis	3 819	–
Total	+ 388	– 1 863

Source: Rezende et al., (1994)

Appendix 1

Brief Summary of Brazil's Basic Statistics

1. Land area... 8 512 000km²

2. Population 1994 (estimated) ....160 million

3. Population growth (1983–8)............................... 2.2 per cent

4. Life expectancy (all groups)................................ 65 years

The economy

5. GDP 1994 – estimated (US$ billion) 375

6. Economic growth (annual, 1980–8) .... 12.4 per cent

7. Inflation (annual, 1984–9) .... 390 per cent

8. Foreign debt (billion $) 114.6

9. Land use (1987), per cent

   Arable land 9.2
   Pasture land.. 19.2
   Forests and woodland...................................... 66.0
   Others 3.2

10. Agricultural output (1987), M tonnes

    Cereals 42.5
    Meat.. 4.7
    Vegetables 5.5
    Fruit.. 27.5

11. Energy (1992), Mtoe.

    Production of primary energy 151.8
    Non-renewables... 40.3
       Oil 31.7
       Others 5.6

    Renewable Sources 111.5

       Hydro 64.7
       Wood/charcoal 24.7
       Sugarcane (ethanol, etc) 19.6

Others 2.4

12. Road and railway network (1988)

    Road (10^6 km) 1.7
    Vehicle fleet (million) 16.6
    Railways (thousand) 22.1

Compiled from: BEN, (1993) and the *Economist*, (1990)

Appendix 2

Some Problems with Measuring Wood and Charcoal

Measuring wood and charcoal is not easy given the many variables involved. A few methods have been developed to analyse the raw materials and products of the charcoal-making process, including sample preparation techniques and the testing of physical properties and chemical analysis, details of which can be found in cited sources. Chemical analysis is particularly important. For example, to find the gross calorific value of a charcoal sample, a known quantity is burned under strictly controlled conditions in oxygen to ensure complete conversion of the charcoal to its combustion products. The heat released by this combustion is determined on the basis of the following equation:

Heat release = mass of sample $\times$ specific capacity of the apparatus $\times$ temperature rise.

The moisture content of a charcoal sample (this represents the water that is physically bound in it) can be found by driving off free moisture from a sample in an oven and recording the mass loss.

Charcoal is usually measured by volume, e.g. m^3, stere or solid stack, or by weight, e.g. tonne, kg, of air or oven dry. The weight of charcoal depends on the moisture content and on the density of the parent wood, assuming it has been completely or near completely carbonized. Weight is the preferred measurement of the most modern charcoal producers.

Charcoal efficiency can be defined either in terms of *weight* or *energy*.

$$Weight = \frac{\text{charcoal output (kg)}}{\text{wood input (kg)}}$$

$$Energy = \frac{\text{charcoal output (MJ)}}{\text{wood input (MJ)}}$$

It is important to note that the heating value of the primary end product (charcoal in this case) is determined by its carbon content. The formulae for the relationship between carbon content (C) and HHV (higher heating value), on dry basis, of combustible fuels is given as follows:

$$HHV = 0.437 \times C - 0.306 \text{ (MJ/kg)}.$$

Converting charcoal to roundwood equivalent.

Three major problems arise if charcoal is converted back to roundwood equivalent: wood density, moisture content of the wood and conversion method, all of which need to be known before comparison calculations can be carried out. The density of the wood governs the yield of charcoal and thus a given volume of charcoal will give different weights of charcoal, depending on the species, moisture content, technology, etc. Moisture content also has an important effect on the yield of charcoal; as noted above the drier the wood the greater the yield of charcoal. The method used to produce charcoal can also affect the yield considerably.

Some conversion figures of wood and fuelwood

(Air dry, 20 per cent moisture)

1 tonne wood	=	1 000kg
(oven dry)	=	$1.38m^3$
	=	0.343t oil
	=	3.5 barrels oil
	=	3.5Mkcal
1t wood (air dry)	=	15GJ
1t wood (oven dry)	=	20GJ
$1m^3$ wood (stacked)	=	0.276 cord (stacked)
1 cord (stacked)	=	$2.12m^3$ (solid)
1 stere* wood (solid)	=	$1m^3$ (0.725t)
1 pile wood	=	0.510t (510kg) (solid)
1t charcoal	=	derived from 4–12t wood**
$1m^3$ charcoal	=	$8.3 – 16.6m^3$ wood
$1m^3$ charcoal	=	0.250t
1kg dry wood (air dry)		produces $1.9–2.2m^3$ producer gas
1kg charcoal		produces $4.2–4.7m^3$ producer gas

---

* Cord and Stere measures can vary appreciably in actual practice
** This wide variation is a result of a number of factors such as species, moisture content, wood density, charcoal piece-size, fines, etc. The range for average tropical hardwoods at 15 per cent moisture content, for example, can be from about $4m^3$ per tonne in a poorly designed kiln. See Table 4.1.
(Note: These are approximate figures only and hence it is important that all conversion factors used are clearly stated).

Sources: Bialy J. (1986); Emrich W. (1985); Hollingdale et al. (1991); Openshaw K. (1983).

www.ingramcontent.com/pod-product-compliance
Ingram Content Group UK Ltd.
Pitfield, Milton Keynes, MK11 3LW, UK
UKHW022113290526
12796UKWH00006B/485